LET LOVE ARISE

40 SHORT ESSAYS

Randall Tremba

Marrisa

Intake Meeting $160

$125/session

Packages

pre-purchase

~~20 sessions $2250~~

$1125

20 | 2250

Published by Four Seasons Books
114 W. German Street
Shepherdstown, West Virginia 25443
Phone: 304.876.3486
Website: fourseasonsbooks.com

Printed in the United States of America by
HBP, Inc., Hagerstown, MD, May 2019

In Praise of *LET LOVE ARISE...*

Tremba's essays—wise and entertaining, filled with good will toward humans everywhere—are a balm, but never an anesthetic, for the mind and spirit. Here's a writer who believes in our better angels. When you read *Let Love Arise,* those angels feel close at hand.

— STEPHEN ALTMAN,
Editor, *Good News Paper*

In these essays Tremba invokes a deep reverence for this planet, something we all must discover if we hope to save our common home. With wit and wisdom he heals the divide between science and religion, reminding us that in this web of life, we all belong to one another.

— MARY ANNE HITT,
Director, Sierra Club Beyond Coal Campaign

For 40 years Tremba wrote essays for the *Good News Paper.* They were well written, thoughtful, insightful, sometimes challenging, sometimes infuriating but always well worth the read. Enjoy and let your spirit be moved.

— THE REV. DR. GT SCHRAMM,
Rector, Trinity Parish, Shepherdstown

For those of us who are spiritual but not necessarily "churchical," Tremba has been a broad, universal, and eminently accessible voice. He speaks the truths of being human in a sometimes inhuman world and touches us with his kind, humble, and humorous soul.

— Hali Taylor,
Director, Shepherdstown Public Library

Tremba's essays are a beguiling combination of accessible prose and scintillating intelligence. Running the gamut from St. Francis of Assisi to Darwin and the gantlet of sex, drugs, and the environment, the good pastor unites these themes with love and humility.

— Mark Madison,
Historian, U.S. Fish and Wildlife Service

Many have anticipated this book for years. It is most gratifying to have it in hand now. It percolates with the wit, wisdom, and compassion of the community-shaping mind and heart of this exemplary imaginative citizen.

— Ed Zahniser,
Shepherdstown Poet Laureate

DEDICATION

To all those readers who've read the

GOOD NEWS PAPER *for forty years or just*

once or twice. Without you it would all be pointless

like a tree falling in the woods with no one around

to hear it. (Or something like that).

TABLE OF CONTENTS

PREFACE

People tell me I'm a good writer and that I should write a book. Well, I don't know about that. I've read too many good writers to think I'm one.

But I am a writer. After all, I have been writing most of my life. Hundreds of term papers and book reports. A doctoral dissertation. Two thousand sermons. A hundred or more stories and skits for the Rumsey Radio Hour. And an essay every three months for the GOOD NEWS PAPER (GNP) for nearly 40 years.

Lots of writing but never a book.

I can't write a book, I told a friend nagging me to do just that after my retirement. To which he replied: No one writes a book. You write a chapter and then another and just keep going until those chapters add up to a book.

Well, if that's true, I'd already written a book and just didn't know it. "Finding Home," "The Flag & Senator Robert Byrd," "Reefer Madness," "Jesus Bugs Me" and "The End of the World" sure sound like chapter titles to me. And so—to commemorate the GNP's 40th anniversary—*Let Love Arise: 40 Short Essays* was conceived and hereby delivered into your hands.

These essays were written over a period of 20 years. Except for the first one ("Finding Home") they are in chronological order. Some address issues, events or prominent people current at that time. So please note the publication date above each chapter title.

ACKNOWLEDGMENTS

A lot of people deserve credit for making this book possible. First and foremost, my long-time friend and co-founder of the GNP—the prolific, prophetic poet Ed Zahniser. Ed's off-the-cuff witticisms alone could fill a book but one stands out to me: *there's no limit to the good that can be done in this world as long as you don't care who gets the credit.* Well, fine. But Ed gets a lot of credit for this publication even if he doesn't want it.

Next is Elizabeth "Libby" Howard. For nearly 20 years she has scoured every essay, gently yet firmly pointing out grammatical or logical flaws, giving me options to better express my befuddled notions and finally smoothing out the spelling, syntax and grammar to perfection. She could make mud readable.

Over the past decade, John Snyder, president of HBP in Hagerstown, Maryland, has graciously made his staff available for the final, pre-press design of the GNP. Twenty years ago, John "reluctantly" agreed to sponsor my Rumsey Radio Hour (RRH) and he's been the "reluctant sponsor" ever since. It says so right on the program cover. So naturally I went to him with my book proposal. Without hesitation or reluctance (as far as I could tell) he agreed to take it on. His design crew at HBP, especially Lori Schulman, deserve a lot of credit for assembling a hodge-podge of puzzling pieces into a handsome format.

And finally, I want to acknowledge the Shepherdstown Ministerial Association (SMA) which 40 years ago saw the potential of an inter-church newsletter to express our unity—"many congregations, one church." The name was a title created "for no particular reason" by Ed Zahniser.

GOOD **SHEPHERDS**
GOOD **TOWN**
GOOD **NEWS PAPER**

A thousand copies of the first issue were hand distributed to the eight town churches in May 1979. By the very next issue it morphed into a community wide, quarterly tabloid magazine which now prints 13,000 copies, is read by approximately 20,000 people and has endured these 40 years as "free, but not cheap" thanks to countless volunteers and generous financial donations from its readers and the Shepherdstown business community. I am grateful that the SMA gave me the opportunity and a platform to hone my voice as a "public theologian."

FOREWORD

Randy Tremba's commitment to lifetime learning convinced me it would be a privilege to try to grow alongside him. This was late 1977, at an all but snowed-out Bible study. I was new to Shepherdstown. Our association has led to a cherished personal and spiritual friendship. Being Randy's friend and sometime co-conspirator in making good things happen in our remarkable community has been a treasured gift. The wild popularity of Randy's recent Life Long Learning classes at Shepherd University confirms that many, many folks recognize Randy's unflagging drive to grow intellectually and to bring us along with him.

In early 1979, Randy and I launched a collective newsletter for Shepherdstown churches that soon became the *Good Shepherd's Good Town Good News Paper*. Our longtime two-newspaper town was then recently without a newspaper. The all-volunteer quarterly tabloid paper now prints 13,000 copies, with some national and even international readers. As executive editor, Randy ritually encamped on page three, which essays compose this remarkable book. Here are humor and whimsy but also truth spoken to power. The book samples 40 of some 150 trenchant ruminations that readers came to anticipate and that Randy so faithfully delivered. That these selected essays number 40 pays homage to the *Good News Paper* 40th anniversary in 2019.

Many have anticipated this book for years. It is most gratifying to have it in hand now. It percolates with the wit, wisdom, and compassion of the community-shaping mind and heart of this exemplary imaginative citizen. Give copies of this book to your kids and grandkids as an ethical will, a worthy tutorial for striving always to get things right, with dignity and generous humor.

— Ed Zahniser

FINDING HOME

Ode to Shepherdstown

How does it feel
To be on your own
With no direction home
Like a complete unknown
Like a rolling stone?
— Bob Dylan

I was ordained as a Presbyterian minister in Southern California in September of 1973. I had a bachelor of arts in philosophy from Wheaton College in Illinois. I had a master's of divinity degree from Fuller Theological Seminary in Pasadena, the most prestigious evangelical seminary in the world. I had a promising career ahead.

And then nine months after my ordination, the world I counted on ended. I lost the love of my life. Heaven and earth collapsed. I tumbled into an abyss.

Over the next six months my body kept going, but my spirit was as good as dead. I trekked through Canada and then across Europe, looking for something I never found. When I came back to the States, I drove aimlessly about, staying with friends and relatives here and there. Still looking for something I couldn't name.

And then in late November 1974, 40 years ago, on a whim, I took a rambling route from my cousin's home in Washington, D.C., to my parents' home in Youngstown, Ohio, for Thanksgiving. That rambling route happened to carry me across the Potomac and Shenandoah rivers at Harpers Ferry. And there I saw something I'd never seen before—the Blue Ridge Mountains and those legendary rivers swirling together. And just like that, something clicked.

On a hunch—and with no other place to call home—I rented a room in a large house across from the Fort Drive-In Theater on Route 340 and took a job as a pruner for Walnut Hill apple orchard. It paid $1.25 an hour.

I had never been so alone.

I was outside nearly every day, often in the freezing cold. I worked with a group of good-hearted, hardscrabble, chain-smoking, illiterate men. And somehow my broken spirit began to heal. I was 27 years old. One of those men took note of my sorry status and suggested I check out Shepherdstown where, as he put it, co-eds abound.

And so, on a cold December day with a light snow falling, I drove for the first time across the thrilling and treacherous Halltown Pike into Shepherdstown—not to check out co-eds so much as to check out a rumor, a rumor of a quaint and charming small town nestled beside the Potomac.

I turned left off Princess Street onto German Street and thought I'd driven onto a movie set—two compact blocks of 19th-century storefronts and sundry rooflines. After a 25-cent cup of coffee at Betty's, I walked around and came upon the Presbyterian church. I opened the front door and walked in.

At that point in my life, I had been in so many different churches I'd lost count. And at that particular time, I really wanted nothing more to do with church. I was disillusioned with life in general and the institutional church in particular.

But I was curious. I was curious about this peculiar-looking church; it seemed more like a New England Quaker Meeting House than any Presbyterian church I'd ever seen.

When I opened that door and walked in, it never occurred to me that this was a "church of last resort." But, as it turns out, that's what it was for me.

It was a Saturday. No one else was there. I was alone.

I saw tired blue paint peeling off the walls. I saw a faded, threadbare blue carpet. I saw worn pews—straight and hard.

I saw a foreboding dark mahogany pulpit and behind it two tall chairs and a sofa, all upholstered with black cloth. And I saw the old rugged cross hanging in the arch, dead center.

I should have turned and left.

But I stayed.

I stood under the balcony, trying to take it all in. But, instead, something was taking me in—a certain spirit that, I would learn later, arose from the wounded and dying sons of this nation who lay on that floor and the floors of many other buildings in this generous town in the fall of 1862, bleeding and pleading for mercy and grace.

I was standing on holy ground, in a house of prayer, in a hallowed village.

Sometimes you have to leave home to find it.

As I stood there that cold December day, I had no idea that the church's current pastor would suddenly resign four months later, leaving that church in the lurch. Nor did I know that at his suggestion I would be asked to preach there on Sundays until a "real minister" could be found.

No, I wasn't insulted in the least by that notion. I had no intention of staying with that or any other church. I would stay for a while and then get on with my life.

The congregation was small. But their hearts were big and full of grace. Even though I was a wreck and not much of a preacher, they took me in. They saw more in me than I saw in myself. They cared for me, said nice things about my obtuse, rambling sermons, and unwittingly mended my broken heart.

I couldn't believe what I'd found.

A year went by and still no real minister had been found. I was given some time off. I flew back to California to see old friends, and fell in love with one. I couldn't wait for her to see Shepherdstown and meet the kind and quirky souls of this quaint village.

And so in March 1976, Paula caught a red-eye from San Francisco to Washington, on a one-way ticket and a hunch. We didn't know much about anything or how things would unfold. After all, as James Rumsey once said, heaven only knows how it will all turn out.

Forty years ago this month, a certain small town experienced in the art of tending the wounded took me in and opened a door on a world of grace. I've been trying to repay that debt of love ever since. ❧

SPRING 1998

FOR LOVE OF BASEBALL AND BAPTISM

And when Jesus had been baptized, just as he came up from the water, suddenly the heavens were opened to him and he saw the Spirit of God descending like a dove and alighting on him. And a voice from heaven said, "This is my son, the Beloved, with whom I am well pleased."
— MATTHEW 3:16–17

My argument with my father about baptism is over. He died December 27, the day before his 84th birthday. It was his last home run.

I was by his bedside the hour he died. We talked. But not about baptism or baseball.

In fact, he didn't talk so much as look. He looked mostly at my mother, his wife of 60 years. The look was fierce, not with anger but with aching—an aching, I suspect, to speak of love one more time. But his lips could not say what his heart held, a heart re-mended time and time again by the balm of Gilead and the grace of a woman who let him win every argument.

My father was a believer. A rascally believer, but a believer nonetheless. He believed baseball players should run their butts off even when they hit a routine fly ball to the outfield. That's what he did. And one time, just one time in about 10,000 times at bat, he dove headfirst safely into third base after the outfielder dropped the ball. For that *one time* I was never allowed to slack on the base path.

He taught me the game. I became a Little League All-Star in Youngstown without ever doing one thing right. "Can't you compliment your son for something," my mother would beg him after innumerable games. *Well,* he said ever so reluctantly after one game, *he struck out with the bases loaded, but he had a pretty good swing at the ball.*

I rode that compliment for years.

My dad was not happy with the modern state of Major League Baseball. *If a man is paid a million dollars and can't bunt, it's a crime,* he'd say. *That guy should be in prison. He's a fraud.*

My father had been in prison once, sort of. Not for missing a bunt but for riding a train.

It was a story he only told (and retold) in his final years. At first I was shocked that the man our mother thought was flawless had been in prison. But I quickly came to respect him even more, even if it was a low crime.

It was the Depression. Jobs were scarce in the coal mines of western Pennsylvania. He was 19, fresh out of high school, and tired of the cold. He and his cousin hopped a train in Connellsville, rumbled through Hagerstown and Baltimore and right into the yards of Raleigh where a railroad cop nailed those freewheeling hobos.

Off they went to a state prison farm. But, hey, it was a job and it came with free room and board. A month later they headed for the deep South seeking jobs, women, and a good game of baseball.

My dad was lucky. He found a baseball game in Decatur that came with a job in a textile company that intended to beat the pants off its rival company in the fiercely competitive industrial league. My dad knew nothing about textiles, but he could rip a ball a mile and tear up the base path. One look at his swing and they hired him.

Too bad he was the only northern guy on the team. "Play that northern boy," his teammates told the manager, "and you'll be sorry."

So my dad had to sit on the bench until the manager was so shorthanded one game that he had to put him in, and my dad just had to go out there and hit for the cycle (single, double, triple, home run), and so the manager just had to sit him back down on the bench again, otherwise he would have been very sorry indeed.

A certain professional baseball scout for the Washington Senators in the stands had seen enough. He offered my dad a contract. It was his lucky break.

But he never got to use it.

He never got to the tryouts. He never got to the majors. He never got to show the big boys how to drop a sweet bunt or beat a triple out of a routine fly ball. Lucky for Cal Ripken. Otherwise Cal would still be chasing "The Streak."

On the First Day of the Rest of His Life, my dad got sick—pneumonia or something. He looked at his bride, he looked at the long tempestuous road ahead, he looked at his life, and stayed home. His family, when it came, would come first. Baseball would be a pastime.

With his southern bride in hand, he took his leave of the South, and took a job with the Pittsburgh and Lake Erie (P&LE) Railroad (which obviously hadn't done a background check on a certain former hobo). They paid him a decent wage, which got better and better as the union got stronger and stronger.

He would later criticize union leaders for getting fat and cozy with management. But to his dying day he'd say, *a bad union is better than no union at all because the rich man never respects the working man.* As a child he had heard about his uncle who had been labeled a communist and blackballed for trying to organize a coal miner's union in West Virginia.

Which, strangely enough, is exactly what my father did to Martin Luther King Jr. *That commie,* he'd say. *He's a traitor to his country.* But, Dad, I'd say, he's a Baptist minister and you're a Baptist. That's when I learned in no uncertain terms that all Baptists are not the same. *He's a disgrace to the name of Jesus Christ. He's trying to ruin this nation.*

That's not why my dad recanted his Baptist (full-body immersion) baptism. For many years he was proud to be a Baptist because the Baptists read the Bible better than the Lutherans. *It says right in the Bible,* he'd say, *that Jesus "came up from the water" which means he must have been "under" or "in" the water not merely "sprinkled" by the hand of John the Baptist.*

He was right about that. The New Testament Greek word for baptism literally means "immersion."

My dad liked to figure things out. The best grip on a boxcar, the best grip on a bat, the best grip on the Bible. He figured this baptism thing out at about age 30, recanted his Lutheran (infant sprinkling) baptism, and dove headfirst into the Bible.

My dad loved baseball, Jesus, the Bible, and (for a while) Carl McIntire (a renegade Presbyterian minister who thought Joe McCarthy was America's greatest patriot). When I came home from college in the Summer of Love, my dad met me at the door wearing a "Victory in Viet Nam" T-shirt.

Everywhere else it was the Summer of Love. In our house it was war. We argued about civil rights. We argued about the Vietnam War. We argued about hair. We argued about baptism.

By then my father, while still a brakeman on the railroad, had become a kind of self-taught, Talmudic scholar of the Bible. He had sent away for books, studied charts, delved into numerology (the 70 weeks of Daniel's prophecy), apocalypticism (The Rapture and Blessed Hope), and came up a full-fledged hyperdispensationalist.

He didn't call it hyperdispensationalism. That's what its critics and scoffers (like me) called it.

As far as I could tell there were only five people on earth who understood the stuff. (Now there are four.)

*Baptism is **inappropriate** for the church, he'd say. The true church doesn't need it, doesn't use it. It's legalism. You've got to **rightly divide the Word** and stop using the Lord's prayer. Forget God's kingdom. It's not coming the way you think it is. God deals with us by grace alone. **Grace.** It's all grace. It's by grace that we are saved, not by works, not by civil rights marches, nor by baptism. It's by grace and grace alone. **Period.***

Ironically, we, his family, had to work very hard to gain his approval. His judgments were harsh. A car mechanic who lied once would never see him again. He didn't see much gray in life.

Grace, it's all by grace, he would say over and over again. And now that he's gone, I suspect grace is the one thing he longed for most. And longed most to give.

He spent hundreds of hours etching a panorama of biblical dispensations on a six foot long scroll of cloth. (Michelangelo didn't treat the Sistine chapel with more care.) I'd study his byzantine chart and shake my head. Dad, I'd say, it's beautiful but wrong. You really missed the ball there, Dad.

He'd smile paternalistically (how else?) and keep sketching just the way I'd smile sophomorically (how else?) at his objections and keep marching for civil rights and against war.

So, I say to myself, so he was wrong about baptism and war and Martin Luther King Jr. He still loved me and I still loved him. And to honor him I sure don't have to be just like him.

That's where baptism comes in.

On January 2, exactly one week after my father's death, I found myself visiting the Martin Luther King Jr. Center in Atlanta. I had planned the visit months before.

Obviously, I wasn't there to honor my father's memory. I was there to honor another memory, a memory of immersion into the Love of God. It's a memory of full body immersion, not into water but into the Name: *How can you say you love God whom you haven't seen, when you fail to love your neighbor whom you have seen.*

So, for now, I get the last word.

Baptism as a sacrament or an ordinance or a rite of the church—baptism by sprinkling, or pouring, or immersion in water—is one thing, and a pretty good thing at that. But immersion (yes, the Baptists got *that* word right!), immersion in the Name of God is something else entirely.

It's there that we hear our own name called.

You are my beloved son, is what Jesus heard when he "came up" to stand on his own two feet. To hear and believe such a thing is powerful. It fills our hearts with love, turns our lives around, and sets them on holy ground, for the moment.

When we are loved we in turn can love others. And love multiplies.

No wonder Jesus said at the end: *As you go into all the nations, among people everywhere, immerse them in the Name of the Father, Son and Holy Spirit.* And when you get down to it, if that Name's not love, what is it? And if it doesn't make us all brothers and sisters, what good is it? And if you can't see it today, perhaps you should go under again.

True baptism is a daily thing.

I've struck out on that path. ❧

SUMMER 2002

ONE PLANET. TWO WORLDS.

My last essay on this page was one year ago. Since then I have been around the world. Thanks, in part, to a grant from the Lilly Endowment and the generous support of the Shepherdstown Presbyterian Church, Paula and I have been to New Zealand, Australia, South Africa, Kenya, Ethiopia, Egypt, Greece, Italy, Spain, France, England, and Ireland. We headed west and kept moving more or less westward—by plane, boat, and train—for 100 days until we arrived back where we started.

I can tell you this: *the earth is round*. I know, I know, you're saying to yourself: 100 days, 12 countries, thousands of dollars later, and that's what he comes back with?

Well, did I mention that the earth is also *big*?

On Wednesday afternoon, September 26, we flew from Dulles to L.A., where the terminal was briefly closed because of a suspected car bomb. (You remember those days, I'm sure.) That night we left L.A. on a Qantas flight that cruised for 12 hours at a speed of nearly 600 mph over nothing but ocean until it landed on a relatively small piece of land called New Zealand. We then took a short flight to Christchurch on New Zealand's south island, where less than a million humans live. On our third day there, we drove west through snow-capped, alpine mountains and two hours later were driving through a rain forest.

We drove north for several days, boarded a ferry, drove another day or two before arriving in Auckland, near the top of the north island. All this on what's called "a small island country."

We flew from New Zealand to Australia, three hours over (again) nothing but ocean. After a week on the east coast of Australia we flew to the west coast—five hours over desert. Australia is a huge island continent with a few million people (and about a zillion kangaroos), living primarily along its outer edges.

A week later we flew from Australia to South Africa, eight hours at nearly 600 mph over (again) nothing but ocean. The earth is covered by more water than I had ever imagined. As someone said: Our planet could have been called "Water" instead of "Earth."

As it turns out, we're very lucky to have a place to stand. We could all have been fish! But we're not, and a whole lot of other species aren't either.

The earth is round, big, and *fantastically diverse.*

Every little thing plays a crucial role in the survival and ongoing evolution of life. Compared to everything that preceded us by millions and millions of years, we humans have been on earth for about two minutes. It behooves us not to think too highly of ourselves—or too lowly. Every little thing plays a crucial role in the web of life. It behooves us to learn how to fit in, respect and trust the force or forces that have brought life to this planet to this point *without our assistance.*

We really should consider the lilies of the field, the birds of the air, whales, rain forests, glaciers, the cliffs of Moher, dung beetles, fungi, algae, minerals, and maggots. If the Maker of heaven and earth meticulously designed such as these why, then, should we fret or be anxious? *Mindfulness* is the way to live, and yet many of us plunge through each day, year after year, *mindlessly*—minding nothing but our manners.

In southwest Australia, we saw critters and other things thriving on the carcass of a 300-year-old Kerri tree that had been dead for 50 years. What does that tell us? At least this much: Life and death are part of the same web. Apparently, everything on this planet is eventually eaten in one way or another and then transformed—resurrected, we might say—to new life. Chew on that for a while.

In life and in death we belong to the whole fantastic work and web of creation and to the One who calls and nudges it into being—eon by eon, glacial age by glacial age, year by year, day by day, minute by minute, second by second. We belong to being itself.

We belong to the Great Spirit, to that which we barely understand, and yet confess or guess to be the Maker of heaven and earth. The Great Spirit is in relationship not only with us, but with the whole earth, as surely as a parent is related and involved with its child. Christians at their best (which isn't too often) want to claim that the Great Spirit is very much like "Jesus," who kept on and kept on enlarging the guest list at his table, a table that many people wanted and still want to fence in. And yet, without diversity there would be no life. The more diversity, the better for all of us.

And the more sharing of life the better.

Everywhere we went, we heard that the world had changed dramatically in one day. For a long time to come, people were saying, September 11 will be the reference point for the division between the way the world was and the way the world has become. Well, that may be true for the world we know, but, as it turns out, there is more than one world on this one planet. One world is in hurry to save itself from destruction. For the other world it's almost too late.

In Cairo, a Muslim tour guide told us that Osama bin Laden had ruined his life and the life of 10 million Egyptians. Business was down, way down, he said, since Americans were afraid to travel. And when Americans don't travel, he said, money isn't spent. And when money isn't spent, his family and millions like his suffer. What clout Americans have!

To be sure, money is not the absolute measure of life; but it is one measure. And by that standard, many people in Ethiopia and Kenya, and countries like them, are poor and getting poorer, even though they work very, very hard.

They are poor, in some cases, because their own government leaders are corrupt, hoarding or misusing money that was intended to build schools, clinics, factories, and infrastructure. In others cases they are poor because our nation, and nations like ours, have rigged the world economy to sustain our high and comfortable standard of living, quietly draining natural and human resources from those countries to benefit our own. We may think we've pulled a fast one, but the rest of the world knows our dirty little secret.

During my travels, I began to wonder just what had united the so-called first world after September 11? What was "the worldview" that trumped all religious and political differences overnight? After the prayer services, what was the tool of salvation we turned to to save "our world?" Pay close attention to that if you want to know what people in the "first world" *really believe* despite various religious affiliations.

It's amazing what humans can do when they put their hearts, minds, and wallets to it. While the "first world" frantically (and brilliantly!) rallies to eliminate international terrorism, who is rallying to eliminate poverty and diseases, which kill more than 3,000 people a day in the third world?

Judgment and grace often arrive together. ❧

THE BEGINNING OF WISDOM

(In remembrance of my mother)

A merry heart does good, like medicine,
But a broken spirit dries the bones.
— Proverbs 17:22

I once let loose of my mother's hand in the basement of a bustling department store in Youngstown, Ohio. Her face vanished into a sea of strangers. I held my breath. I spun round and round, searching and searching, sinking into primal darkness. Just before my heart stopped, she found me and grabbed my hand. I was three years old and that was my first experience of salvation.

This past spring my mother let loose of my hand for good. But she left plenty for me to hold on to.

At age seven, alone in the basement on a rainy day, I was wondering what those newfangled electric washer ringers might do to my soaking wet Roy Rogers cowboy gloves. I found out. The grinders easily accepted the wet glove (and my hand, which I had left in the glove), slowly rolled over my wrist, and began crawling toward my elbow, which (as anyone knows) leads to the shoulder, which leads to the neck, which leads to… THE HEAD! I screamed and, just like that, mom leapt down 12 steps and pulled my arm and hand free from the clutches of death. Again.

Six years later, I became a teenager and wanted nothing to do with my mother. I was thoroughly ashamed of her and my father. *How in the world did I end up with the worst parents on earth? Why me, Lord?!*

Case in point: While I ate breakfast before going to school every morning she would read a Bible verse to me and expound its relevance to life, specifically my life. Her favorite by far was the Book of Proverbs. *The fear of the LORD is the beginning of wisdom.* I heard *that* a thousand times. And this one almost as much: *You don't prove your love to a woman by going to bed with her; you prove your love to her by getting out of bed and going to work.* I'm pretty sure she made that one up.

When I began seventh grade she took a job as a women's shoe clerk in a department store to earn money for my college education. For her, college was the Promised Land. But as much as she respected education she was wary of it, too. Education is a good thing, she once told me, *as long as you don't let it go to your head.* That, as you might guess, is a little tricky.

During my sophomore year (the year we finally surpass our parents in knowledge!) I discovered Sigmund Freud. (I had read one part of one chapter from one book, at least!) I couldn't wait to tell my mother how parents mess up their children *badly.* She listened intently with utter, jaw-dropped amazement. *Brilliant,* she exclaimed, obviously pleased how much college had done for me so far. Y*our generation is simply brilliant,* she said again. *My generation was simply too ignorant to know we could blame our parents.* Brilliant, just brilliant, she muttered as she left me sitting at the kitchen table alone with all my knowledge.

My mother grew up in Alabama. Her father was often absent, which made her mother's and siblings' lives extremely hard. She quit school after the eighth grade to work for pen*nies in a textile mill.* If life gives you lemons make lemonade. That was one of her favorite expressions. And this: *Don't curse the darkness; light a candle.* And this: *Keep looking up. Grief, resentment, and bitterness will kill your spirit if you let them,* she said over and over again. *Don't wallow in the past. Be open to the future.*

Shortly after my father died, I asked my mother how she was coping (not one of her favorite words or concepts). *Good enough,* she replied. *He's dead. There's nothing I can do about it. I miss him. But there's no use moping the rest of my life. I got things to do.* And she did them all with gusto until her body gave out on May 31.

My mother died at my sister's home in Florida at age 92, three days before my son's wedding in Albuquerque. I told my son and daughter-in-law that my mom once told me the first five years of marriage were the toughest, and when I reminded her of that a few years ago, she said: *Did I say that? I meant 50!* She and my father were married 60 years before he died nine years ago.

My father was a patient man, up to a point. His scoldings were few but harsh. Hardly ever did my mother contradict my father, or he her, in front of their children, with one exception. When my father scolded me about botching something, she'd say quietly, *Mike, don't scold. Teach. Don't scold. Show him how to do it right.*

Once during my senior college year, I returned home with a full beard and shoulder-length hair. It was "the Sixties," remember, and it's what all of us white boys did to prove we were individuals. My mother opened the door, screeched, and ran to the back of the house. She spent the next three days pleading, scolding, or bribing me to shave. But I had too much pride and integrity to give in. (Not to mention a girlfriend who really dug my long hair!)

To console my mother I invited her into the living room to inspect the one and only picture allowed to hang in our house. It was the "classic" picture of Jesus knocking on a door. He was wearing a flowing robe and sandals and sporting a beard and beautiful shoulder-length hair. Mom, I said. Look! Jesus has a beard and long hair. My mother studied the picture for a few minutes then looked at me and said: *It's easy to look like Jesus.*

On the first day of my second grade, she had planned to walk with me and sit through opening exercises as she had done when I began first grade. But this is *second* grade, I told her. And I am perfectly capable of walking two blocks and finding my desk *all by myself.*

She let me go alone.

I walked into my new homeroom and slowly noticed that *all the other children* had a mother with them. I was the only orphan. I bolted out the door and ran home as fast as I could fly. My mother got herself ready without a word, took my hand, and walked with me back to the school.

It would take many, many years for me to appreciate that little mustard seed of love: the grace of mere presence, the deep solace of a fellow human being sitting with another when we are afraid to be alone. And when you think about it, our only hope of loving someone else is not because we have read a book or heard a lecture or a sermon. We love others because we have been loved first. We love others because someone once held our hand when we were lost. ❧

WINTER 2006

WHO WOULD JESUS BOMB?

Jesus went on with his disciples to the villages of Caesarea Philippi; and on the way he asked his disciples, "Who do people say that I am?"
—Mark 8:27

~

The bumper sticker: *Who would Jesus bomb?* is both silly and provocative. Silly because Jesus lived before bombs, as we know them, were invented. Provocative because "Jesus," even in popular culture, remains the standard or symbol for right behavior. That question (*Who would Jesus bomb?*) and those like it are shorthand ways of asking—not merely what is the *right* thing to do—but what is the *absolutely* right thing to do in any given situation.

That is the edge on the name of "Jesus" in such a question.

It began with: *What would Jesus do?* And now we have: What would Jesus *drive*? Where would Jesus *shop*? And we could add: Where would Jesus *live*? What would Jesus *wear, eat, chew, and drink*?

I've got a few unauthorized answers.

Jesus would drive a scruffy Japanese pickup truck. Why? Because *I* drive a scruffy Japanese pickup. He would shop at Wal-Mart and not at Saks Fifth Avenue. Why? Because Jesus likes to mix and mingle with ordinary, hard-working people trying to get by on very little. Where would he live? In a

McMansion. Why? Because he said, "In my Father's house are many mansions." See how much fun this can be?

Who would Jesus bomb?

I once thought there was only one Christian answer to that question, but I was wrong.

Twenty-some years ago while visiting my parents in Englewood, Florida, my mother, a tenacious Baptist, insisted that I attend a Presbyterian church that she had discovered and liked. She especially liked the young, handsome, dynamic minister who, as she put it, preached the pure and simple gospel from the Bible *without bringing in politics*—and then she poked her finger in my chest and said: *the way you do.* My mother had read a few of my sermons and didn't like my political slant.

The young, handsome, dynamic minister's lesson for the day was from "the Sermon on the Mount." *Love your enemies.* Well, I thought, there is only one way this can turn out. I was wrong. When he got to the part about "turning the other cheek," he noted that Jesus meant turn it *once* and then if your enemy's belligerence persisted you were free to *clobber him with everything you had.* Now that's a novel interpretation, I thought.

It got even better.

By the end of the sermon he was urging his congregation to get behind President Reagan's fledgling defense program by signing a petition available in the vestibule. We sang a hymn and the service was over.

A line formed to sign the petition and another to shake the minister's hand at the exit. I bit my tongue, shook his hand, and got into my parents' car. WOW, mom, I said, your minister sure preaches *the pure and simple gospel!* To which my mother replied: *OK, OK, that was a mistake.*

It was some comfort to me to note that particular church belonged to a different Presbyterian denomination from my own. That denomination also believes Jesus would not ordain women as ministers. Not all Presbyterians are alike. And not all Christians are alike. For instance, we read the Bible differently.

Who would Jesus bomb? A certain church in a certain town in Florida had an answer, and I'm pretty sure it wasn't the only church preaching that answer then or now.

President Truman was a devout Christian and decided it was better to bomb Hiroshima, better to kill many civilians all at once to save many, many more of *Truman's favored people*. It was a horrible but necessary calculus, or so he believed.

That calculus seems reasonable to many of us. But, then, what of Saddam Hussein, who justified using poisonous gas against his Kurdish enemies with the same calculus? Saddam was fed up with the 10-year-long, costly war with Iran. Saddam, too, wanted a quick end to the endless killing *of his favored people*.

What is the right thing to do, the *absolutely right thing* to do when those you love are being led like sheep to the slaughter? *What would Jesus do?*

Dietrich Bonhoeffer, the 20th-century German Lutheran pastor and theologian who wrote the book *Cost of Discipleship*, gradually came to embrace pacifism as the way of Jesus. He was one of only a few ministers who refused to preach the Nazi gospel in church. And yet, he conspired with a small cadre of other Germans to assassinate Hitler by hiding a bomb under the führer's table. The attempt failed. Bonhoeffer was arrested, imprisoned, and executed.

Bonhoeffer never claimed that what he did was right. In fact, he thought it might be terribly wrong. All he could do was throw himself upon the mercy of God.

What would Jesus do? Who would Jesus bomb?

Christians have tried to extrapolate from the Bible what Jesus and/or God might say about contemporary issues. The church has gotten it right some times; and wrong some times. The Bible may be necessary but it is not sufficient. New knowledge, insights, and experiences must be taken into account. The mind and heart must be fully engaged.

At one time slavery was justified by appealing to the Bible, as were the subordination of women, and the exclusion of divorced and remarried persons from ordained ministry in the church. And now the church is divided on the question of ordaining persons who are homosexual.

What would Jesus do? Who would Jesus ordain? Who would Jesus bomb?

What makes these questions difficult is that the *Jesus before Easter* and the *Jesus after Easter* are not exactly the same. Jesus said of himself that *the seed must die for the grain to grow.* The seed and the grain are not exactly the same. Indeed, his spirit has outgrown the Jewish husk in which it was first embodied.

Jesus was an innovative Jewish teacher of wisdom. He taught and embodied true communion with the One and true community with others. His passion was for life. And yet he accepted death on a cross as a way to end the perpetual cycle of violence and revenge among his people, or so he believed. It was a radical act of faith—childlike trust that love, not hate, was at the heart of reality.

After Easter, "Jesus" arose in more ways than one, including rising into the collective consciousness of his Jewish followers, and from there across ethnic and national boundaries. Jesus arose in the imagination of countless souls including St. Francis, Teresa of Avila, Gandhi, Mother Teresa, Dorothy Day, and Martin Luther King Jr., to name just a few.

"Jesus," a historic person, has become a symbol and sacrament of undying love. "I will love my enemies even if it kills me." The challenge is not to mimic the first-century Jewish Jesus but to embody that way of love with all the intelligence, wisdom, and courage we can muster in ever-changing situations. "Jesus" is what happens when the divine and human live and work in harmony. And where that happens, the bombing stops and the peacemaking begins. ❧

THE ENDLESS AND POINTLESS QUEST FOR THE LIVING GOD

The God Who Only Knows Four Words

Every
Child
Has known God,
Not the God of names,
Not the God of don'ts,
Not the God who ever does
Anything weird,
But the God who only knows four words
And keeps repeating them, saying:
"Come dance with Me."
Come
Dance.
—Hafiz

I am no scientist, but I am a big fan of science and scientists. Over time, scientists have discovered that every time they get to the bottom of anything tiny, such as cells, molecules, atoms, and quarks, or any time they get to the top of anything big, such as stars, clusters, galaxies, black holes, there always seems to be another layer beneath or above. Reality, as it were, continues to lure us in deeper and deeper. It's why scientists say: *Today's conclusion is tomorrow's premise.* Surprise and serendipity are inevitable in this world. The quest for truth is endless.

Now when Jesus came into the district of Caesarea Philippi, he asked his disciples, "Who do people say that the Son of Man is?" And they said, "Some say John the Baptist, but others Elijah, and still others Jeremiah or one of the prophets." He said to them, "But who do you say that I am?" (Matthew 16:13-15)

Who do you say that I am?

That's one of many questions on the quest for the living God.

Quest for the Living God is a book by Elizabeth Johnson. The quest for the living God is also an adventure. The book is short; the adventure, however, is endless. And pointless.

It's pointless because there really is no quest. You are already there. You are already in and with "God" (for lack of a better name at the moment) for God is Reality, the Ground of our Being, known by many names.

The quest is pointless. It's also endless. Endless because God (to use that name again) is like someone you love, which is to say, incomprehensible. When you love someone, there's always more to discover, more to be revealed as the relationship evolves. Those revelations tend to come in many and various ways.

The quest for the living God is endless also because *complete knowledge* is like the horizon—always a few steps out of reach. You can't get there anymore than you can get to tomorrow.

God may in fact be *That* which lures us ever onward and ever deeper in our quest for knowledge and intimacy. Just think: God as seducer, as bewitcher, as the apple on the tree. *Take, taste, and see. Seek and you shall find. Come know me. Come dance with me. I dare you.*

Who do you say that I am?

Recently, I met with some young adults asking a similar question of themselves. This summer, they had been to places where life was dark and grim and hopeless, especially for innocent children. So each of these students was asking, in one way or another: *In the face of grim situations which I have seen with my own eyes, what ought I to do with my one wild and precious life? How can I bear light into the darkness around me?*

As it turns out, the God of monotheistic tradition is implicated in the darkness. Take the Bible story from Exodus chapter one as an example. What kind of God allows the massacre of babies? If God is all-powerful and all good, why do such things happen? There is no easy answer, but I'm pretty sure the question leads through the cross. For Christians, the cross suggests that the primal force, which was once irresistible has somehow become vulnerable, the way love is vulnerable to rejection. Or crucifixion.

What kind of God allows the massacre of babies? Sometimes it's best to leave God out of it and ask, *What kind of people, what kind of nation, what kind of church allows those things to happen*?

Pharaoh's decree to kill all Hebrew baby boys happened in Egypt long ago. But it wasn't too long ago that 6 million Jews were massacred by the Nazis in a land with thousands of churches. Thousands of churches and millions of Christians! You'd have to have a very hard heart not to reject your faith after that! Or, at least, seriously rethink it!

It's a good thing to think. And rethink. To ask questions and more questions. It's good to question authority and then ask, *Who says: 'question authority'?*

In our rethinking, we must not ignore the Holocaust, the Armenian genocide, or the Killing Fields of Cambodia. Nor the grinding poverty that crushes the life out of millions today in far too many places. Nor the plight of women crippled by patriarchy. Nor the goodness of other religions. Nor the findings of evolutionary biology, anthropology, cosmology, astrophysics, and so much coming out of the field of science.

We must not ignore the insights of atheists like Richard Dawkins (*The God Delusion*), Sam Harris (*The End of Faith*), and Christopher Hitchens (*God Is Not Great*), who, by the way, do us a great favor by convincingly discrediting a god we have no business acknowledging anyway: some aloof, invincible monarch playing tricks with the world. Thank God for atheists!

Being an atheist can be a good thing.

In case you hadn't heard, the first Christians were called *atheists* because they refused to give their allegiance to the popular gods of the Roman Empire, which made them subversive in the eyes of the emperor. It's time again to be known as atheists, especially if God is construed as a LORD who consigns some people to heaven and others to hell based on giving or not giving assent to incredible sectarian creeds and unrealistic claims about the world. It's time again to be known as atheists, especially if that God is countermanding Jesus' command to love our enemies, which (if I may go out on a limb here to say it) probably doesn't mean kill them.

If God is, as the Bible suggests, *in and through all things*, there is nowhere we can be or look that the divine is not present. *The earth is full of the glory of God.* In other words, we touch the divine as we explore and probe the world around us—the world of physics, biology, chemistry, geology, and ecology—the world of relationships, and the world within us. In theology this is called *radical immanence*—God in all things, including the darkness.

In the light of what we've learned over the past 150 years about the Bible itself and in the light of discoveries about cosmology and ecology we can see that "Christ" is not some creed or institution or religion, but rather a nested emergent symbol of a worldwide beloved community, which may in fact be the whole web of life. The "Body of Christ" may be a metaphor for the slow rising of a new species out of the human, a species procreated and sustained by love and compassion for all. If so, each of us has the potential and possibility of living our small precious lives faithfully and lovingly in our given niche, trusting that the outcome will be as glorious as what has arisen and unfolded over billions of years. What a privilege to be included, if only for a moment!

Live, my friends, for the sake of the whole. Live for the sake of the holy as you undertake the endless and pointless quest for the living God.

Be still and know that I am *God*.

Be still and know that *I am*.

Be still and know *that*.

Be still and *know*.

Be *still*.

Be. ❧

WINTER 2007

A DARING ADVENTURE

Security is mostly a superstition. It does not exist in nature, nor do the children of men as a whole experience it. Avoiding danger is no safer in the long run than outright exposure. Life is either a daring adventure or nothing.

—Helen Keller

Sometimes we stumble into the wild. Sometimes we walk in on our own.

Seventeen years ago, a young man named Christopher McCandless walked away from his home and family and right into the wilderness. He was looking for enlightenment. In the end, he lost his life.

Sometimes we stumble into the wild. Sometimes we walk in on our own.

In 1990, Christopher McCandless walked away from his home and family and into the Alaskan wilderness in order to find truth. In the end, he lost his life but found his soul.

Christopher's story is told in a book by Jon Krakauer and in the Sean Penn movie *Into the Wild*. As it turns out, life without soul is not worth living.

After graduating from Emory University, Christopher gave his $24,000 graduate school nest egg to charity, abandoned his car, and set off for Alaska to find his soul in a roundabout way. He left an enclosed world for an undisclosed one.

Sometimes we stumble into the wild. Sometimes we walk straight in.

Sometimes we gain the world and lose our souls. Sometimes we lose the world and gain our souls.

When some were speaking about the temple, saying how it was adorned with beautiful stones and gifts dedicated to God, Jesus said, "These things that you see now, the day will come when not one stone will be left upon another; all will be thrown down."

Christopher left his world of entitlements behind. He left no stone upon another. He left and set out on a daring adventure. Along the way he was befriended by others, others who were broken yet wise. Christopher was embraced by old souls.

At times these old souls thought the young soul stupid and said so—stupid to give up his comfortable and promising world for a life of insecurity and uncertainty. At times they thought him stubborn—stubborn for denying forgiveness to his flawed and fraudulent parents.

At times they thought him heroic. And at times they thought him blessed. Troubled and blessed. These old souls wanted to coddle and cuddle the fledgling one, but Christopher kept on. Unfolding.

Sometimes we lose the world and gain our souls.

We have only begun to imagine the fullness of life. How could we tire of hope? So much is in the bud. **Denise Levertov**

"Christopher" is a name like any other name. But, for what it's worth, it does mean "the one who bears the Christ." Of course, it's not our name that matters most. It's the quest that matters. Whatever our name, we can bear the beams of love on the quest for enlightenment.

In the wild, Christopher found out what souls were meant for. And just like that, he collected himself and his books and turned his face toward home. But the river was wide. The river was deep. The river was impossible.

Life is a daring adventure. We can reduce the danger, but we'll never eliminate it. We can hunker down in our shell, hunker down and avoid the wind, rain, and heat, or we can stretch our wings and risk the flight. We can crave the "holy temples" of the past, or we can look for a new heaven and new earth every day. We can welcome and embrace life's many surprises and knocks. Even death.

There's a thread you follow. It goes among things that change. But it *doesn't change. People wonder about what you are pursuing. You have to explain about the thread. But it is hard for others to see. While you hold it you can't get lost. Tragedies happen; people get hurt or die; and you suffer and get old. Nothing you do can stop time's unfolding. You don't ever let go of the thread.* **William Stafford,** "The Way It Is"

I know, I know. It's easier said than done. So it helps to have a faithful companion or two. And it helps to belong to a community of faith that dares to name the mystery that will never leave us or forsake us. ❧

WINTER 2008

THE JOSHUA GENERATION

A Time for Patriotism

What's called of us in this Joshua generation? What do we do in order to fulfill the legacy; to fulfill the obligations and the debt that we owe to those [of the Moses generation] who allowed us to be here today?

— Barack Obama, Selma, Alabama, March 2007

Our nation is in trouble. Yes, we have reasons to hope. President-elect Obama certainly personifies a new day. But it's not inevitable. It's only possible—possible in a way it's not been for a long, long time.

This is a time for patriotism. This is a time for love of country. This is a time for optimism—be it ever so cautious.

For too long the hand of wickedness has been unrestrained in this land. It's time to strengthen the hand of righteousness again. It's time to give our hearts, minds, and souls to making America a wholesome nation again.

This is a time for patriotism. *Patriotism,* not triumphalism. This is a time to mend. This is a time to re-gather ourselves. This is a time to dance. This is a time to laugh.

When the LORD brought back the captives to Zion, we were like those who dreamed. Our mouths were filled with laughter, our tongues with songs of joy. Then it was said among the nations, "The LORD has done great things for them." The LORD has done great things for us, and we are filled with joy. Those who sowed in tears have reaped with songs of joy. Those who went out weeping, carrying seed to sow, have returned with songs of joy, carrying sheaves with them. (Psalm 126)

Overnight, the face and future of America has changed. Change, as it turns out, was a longing held in the heart of nearly every American, no matter which candidate we supported. For some, that aching had endured for centuries, passed from one generation to the next.

Whether we are children of former slaves or children of former immigrants, whether we are children of pilgrims or children of Native Americans, we have longed as one people to reach the Promised Land, that promise beheld in the vision of our nation's founders, a land that would become ever more *free from* the tyranny of religion, *free from* the tyranny of unrestrained power and wealth, *free from* the tyranny of titles and entitlements and *free for* more diversity, more inclusiveness, more equality, and more opportunities.

In his speech in Selma, presidential candidate Obama paid homage to Martin Luther King Jr.'s generation, that generation and the leaders of that generation who, like the biblical Moses, led a people year after year after year through the wilderness, and finally to the banks of the Jordan River, the edge of the Promised Land. That place embodied all their hopes for freedom, prosperity, and equality. Moses saw it from afar. He never got there.

In his acceptance speech November 4, President-elect Obama extended that singular story to all previous generations of Americans who planted and cultivated the seeds of justice and hope in this fair land. For one shining moment—as that Tuesday night gave way to Wednesday morning—we glimpsed a breathtaking sight: All around the world people were laughing and dancing. The harvest was coming home. As Martin Luther King put it: *The moral arc of the universe is long, but it always bends toward justice.*

This is a Joshua Generation. No matter our age, position, or circumstances, we are part of a new generation given the opportunity to fulfill the promise of this great nation—not as the biblical Joshua did by killing his opponents but in a metaphorical way—by pushing back residual racism and sexism, by pushing back apathy, cynicism, narcissism, pessimism, mean-spiritedness, materialism, greed, and sheer fear, so that more freedom, peace, love, and justice may blossom in this beautiful country.

Twenty-five years ago I had the privilege of driving Mr. Ernest Stutzman, a highly respected professor emeritus of Shepherd College, back to his hometown of Helvetia, West Virginia. At that time he was nearly 90 years old and nearly blind.

We talked of many things along the way, including the condition of our nation. I've never forgotten one particularly poignant remark: *These days,* he said, *the American motto seems to be: Get as much you can, any way you can, as fast as you can.* That was 25 years ago.

It's time for that to stop. This is a time for patriotism. This is a time to give.

Money comes and goes, and who knows what it's really worth? But we do know this: We can still build bridges, cars, boats, trains, planes, museums, libraries, and institutions. We know how to make bread, wine, movies, music, poetry, and much, much more. We know how to educate our children. We know how to research and experiment. We know how to solve problems. We know how to rebound and rebuild after disasters. We know how to care for the sick, the weary, the homeless, the orphan, the bereaved, and the refugee. We know how to fill our homes with goodness in abundance. We know how to make peace instead of war.

And we know how to make and enforce laws that curb human propensities toward evil, like getting rich—filthy rich—at the expense of others. We've done it before. We can do it again.

I appeal to my young readers especially: Give your heart, mind, and soul to making America a wholesome nation again. Serve it well in the private sector or in public service. *Please do not despair of government.* Nearly all government workers are good, decent, hard-working, and competent people. Without smart, good, and righteous government our nation will perish. Please find a way to make America better.

This is no time to think your age or your small job doesn't matter much. Your value cannot be measured by money alone. Life is ecological and holistic. In the web of life the tiny ant is as important as the bald eagle. And the same goes for a nation. Each of us is crucial to the whole.

Whether you're young or old or in between, this is the time to work better. Whatever your job, paid or volunteer, do it just a little better than you've done it before. Take it up a notch. Study hard, work hard, pray hard, play hard. Buy less. Save more. Gripe less. Love more.

America is like a vineyard. We are not the best or greatest in the world. We are but one of many. But this vineyard we call America is ours to cultivate and harvest. There is a lot of good work to do. Our fruits must be the fruits of righteousness, which is to say, freedom, peace, justice, compassion, health, humility, and life in abundance for all our people.

We in the Moses generation know one thing: Opportunities like this don't come often and they don't last forever. The harvest is ready. Are you? ❧

CONFESSIONS OF A WHITE, HETEROSEXUAL, CHRISTIAN MINISTER

Thanks to Jesus, Lincoln, and Darwin

A leper came to Jesus begging him, and kneeling said, "If you choose, you can make me clean." Moved with pity, Jesus stretched out his hand and touched him, and said, "I do choose. Be clean!" Immediately the leprosy left him, and he was made clean.
—The Gospel According to Mark 1:40

It's not easy being me. And I'm sure it's not easy being you. Yes, we are all beloved children of God; nevertheless, we are all wounded, sick, and sinful. I am on the road to recovery thanks to Jesus, Abraham Lincoln, and Charles Darwin.

I grew up scorning people of color as inferior to myself. I scorned homosexuals too, and found them repulsive. It was part of the culture, part of my household, and enforced by the Bible.

My father once opened his Bible and showed me verses in Genesis that proved blacks were cursed by God and destined for slavery. It's a ludicrous interpretation of the Bible, but he and a million other Christians believed it.

It took years, but eventually I realized how unclean, toxic, and infectious I had become. I had said and done many hurtful things to others. Unwittingly, I've spent my adult life in this community seeking redemption through my work of preaching and writing.

I sometimes think God graciously and humorously put me in a pulpit as a form of long-term therapy because I needed an entire congregation to pray for me and because I needed a job that forced me to read and reread the Bible over and over again in order to rid myself of a deadly virus. As it turned out, the very thing that had stricken me as a child would also be my medicine.

I took my leprosy to Jesus, and he put me on the road to recovery.

My mother was born and raised in Alabama. After moving to Ohio she became a born-again Christian, but even that didn't cleanse her of certain prejudices. She once told me she felt sad for black people. Why, Mommy? I asked. Because, she said, they want to be white and can't.

I was about 10 years old at the time. I believed her. She was godlike to me. So when she told me about homosexuality being an abomination unto the Lord, I believed her.

When my mother was still living, and living in Florida, her neighbors happened to be a lesbian couple. She liked them a lot and they her. She was kind to them but, she told me during one of my visits, she was sad for them because she knew they'd rather be heterosexual and have a man for a lover.

I was no longer 10 years old. I didn't believe her. My mother was wrong about that. But to her everlasting credit, she loved those women and did not hate them.

I loved and love my mother dearly. But she turned out to be not so perfect. She was flawed and wounded by certain cultural indoctrinations as we all are. But I wouldn't throw my mother off the train any more than I'd throw out the Bible for containing certain odious cultural practices, such as sanctioning slavery, condoning patriarchy and genocide, or denouncing shrimp-eating and homosexuality as "an abomination unto the Lord." What were they thinking? *Shrimp*?!

Jesus got me on the road to recovery. Abraham Lincoln helped, too.

Lincoln opened new vistas on justice and equality, abolishing demeaning definitions of humanness along with slavery. Lincoln helped me realize that it takes more than arguments from the Bible to see the truth. North and South, he said, read the same Bible while coming to different conclusions about slavery. Lincoln came to the presidency with prejudices against blacks *but his experiences with them* changed his heart.

Jesus got me on the road to recovery. Lincoln helped. So did Charles Darwin.

Darwin opened new vistas on the awesome processes of nature by showing how the earth keeps unfolding as a more and more welcoming place to more variety, more complexity, and more diversity. It's the way of the earth. It's the way of God. Mutations and deviations we fear and deplore often turn out to enrich and strengthen the web of life. If only my mother could have known and understood.

I teach a confirmation class for high school students. Recently we took up the story of creation in Genesis. I asked the students what they had heard about Genesis. Without exception they had heard that you couldn't believe Genesis *and* evolution, too. And without exception they all believe evolution. Therefore, they are not inclined to believe much, if anything, about the Bible or the church. Who can blame them?

Genesis is currently *the single greatest intellectual obstacle to Christian faith*. And that's a crying shame.

I, and many others, believe in Genesis *and* evolution.

I asked the confirmands to consider some facts. Genesis was composed about 3,000 years ago. Before the Genesis story ever existed, human beings had been around for *hundreds of thousands of years*. Don't you think, I asked them, that most humans had figured out the sequential order of the natural world long before there were Bibles or books of any sort?

You don't need Genesis to tell you that you can't have humans without animals first. You can't have big animals without little animals first. You can't have little animals without plants first. You can't have plants without soil. You can't have soil without water and light. This is not rocket science, and that's not the big news in Genesis anyway.

Humans knew that much tens of thousands of years ago. Furthermore, they all assumed there was a god or gods behind it all. Even "God said" is not the big news in Genesis. There are dozens of such ancient creation stories with gods in them.

What, then, is Genesis chapter one about?

It's about the *character* of the Mystery within and beyond the natural world—something science can't prove or disprove. After all, science is only one way of knowing. Poetry is another.

In a dark and foreboding time (about 600 BCE), a Hebrew poet took the universally known sequence of the natural world and compressed it into a familiar, seven-day structure. (We do a similar thing by compressing a billion years of evolution into 24 hours, showing humanity's late arrival, just a minute or so before midnight.) With the "voice of God" as an "off-stage prop," the poet composed an anthem of praise, hope, and faith about the *character of the Mystery* within and behind the natural world, pronouncing every single phase of creation as intrinsically good—from the tiniest to the largest, from the oldest to the most recent.

Yes, I know. Life can be terrifying. But behold, it is good. Be not afraid. Even when you can't prove it, even when it seems unlikely, trust the goodness of my Spirit to make the world and you more and more beautiful, more whole, more holy, and more hospitable. I will heal and redeem you, not overnight but slowly over time as I am trying to do with that wreck of a human writing this essay.

Be not afraid. Revel in life. Enjoy the world. Do good work. Reach out for love, and love will reach out to you. ❧

TO FORGIVE OR NOT

Forgiving is love's revolution against life's unfairness. When we forgive, we ignore the normal laws that strap us to the natural law of getting even and, by the alchemy of love, we release ourselves from our own painful pasts.
— Lewis B. Smedes

If you want to see the brave, look at those who can forgive. If you want to see the heroic, look at those who can love in return for hatred.
— The Bhagavad Gita

Then Peter came and said to Jesus, "Lord, how often should I forgive? Should I forgive someone as many as seven times?" Jesus said to Peter, "No, not seven times; seventy-seven times."
— Matthew 18:21

A woman once asked me if she should forgive her father, a father who had abused her repeatedly as a child. The daughter had eventually escaped his control and threats. The father felt no guilt or remorse. He was, as he proudly proclaimed, a born-again Christian. He maintained that God had forgiven all his sins through the death of Jesus. He had been, as he put it, *washed in the blood of the lamb*. So he didn't need his daughter's forgiveness.

For a decade or more, there had been no communication between father and daughter. But now the father was on his deathbed. He had come to his senses and was longing for forgiveness, not from God this time, but from a certain human being, from the daughter he had badly and deeply hurt. His daughter was now happily married and as far as she was concerned *her father could rot in hell.*

Forgive or not?

In 1942 in Poland, a young Nazi SS trooper was on his deathbed. He had willingly assisted with the cold-blooded murder of hundreds of Jewish men, women, and children. He was now terribly sorry. This man, who had been raised Catholic, longed for forgiveness and absolution. His attending nurse fetched a Jew from a nearby concentration camp and brought him to the Nazi's bedside. The frightened, frazzled, and emaciated Jew listened for hours to the German's detailed confession and then his plea for forgiveness.

Forgive or not?

Is there an American who could ever forgive Osama bin Laden on behalf of the 9/11 victims? Is there an Armenian, a Cambodian, a Tutsi, or an Iraqi who could forgive the perpetrators of unspeakable atrocities inflicted on their people? Who among the poor of the earth will one day forgive Americans—we who are coddled in the belly of an empire? Who among the poor of the earth will one day forgive Americans for remaining silent, busy, and fat while peoples and nations, men, women, and children, were systematically ushered into "death chambers" of another sort?

Forgive or not?

In this town several years ago a man cheated on his wife. The affair was discovered. He asked to be forgiven. His wife forgave him. He cheated again and asked for forgiveness. And again. And again. His wife was a devout Christian and wanted to do the right thing. Seventy-seven times is a lot. Seven times seventy is even more. She knew counting wasn't the point. The point is unlimited forgiveness, sometimes for the same offense.

Forgive or not?

Years ago when I lived in California, a friend said something unkind to me. To this day I can't remember what it was. But

I do remember he asked me to forgive him. Whatever it was it was a minor zinger, the kind we give and get every day, if not every hour. I remember saying to him: *Oh, forget it. It was nothing.* But he wasn't after a brush-off. *No,* he said, looking me straight in the eye, *Let's not forget it. I hurt you. It was wrong. Please forgive me before something small begins to fester.*

Forgive or not?

Forgiveness is a beautiful thing, but it's not a simple thing. Some people don't have the right to forgive or be forgiven. Some people enjoy nursing a wound, a grudge, or resentment. It gives meaning to their lives.

Many people are ready to forgive but if the offender has not asked for forgiveness, then what? Forgiveness is a beautiful thing but it is not simple.

That wife divorced her unfaithful husband. She knew that forgiveness is an infinite obligation; but she also knew that no one is obligated to stay in a marriage if they are beaten over and over or in a business partnership if they are cheated over and over.

That abused daughter forgave her father. Not quickly and not alone. I recommended a professional counselor because in serious situations, sentimental or cheap forgiveness can do more harm than good. It was a treacherous process.

In front of the counselor and in front of his wife (the mother of the abused daughter) that father had to describe in some detail what he had done. The father had to listen to his daughter describe the hurt and shame she had endured and then repeat what she said to make sure he got it, to make sure he understood the size of the debt he was begging her to forgive. The counselor suggested that the daughter give herself time, days if necessary, to consider what, if anything, she would do.

A week later, the daughter who once wished her father would rot in hell found it within herself to forgive. There were no hugs and no kisses. Just a few quiet tears.

The daughter's emotional scars did not disappear. But now, at least, her future is no longer shackled by bitterness, resentment, and victimization. For her, and I suppose for her father, that moment was an exodus from a torture chamber not unlike the Exodus portrayed in the Bible story. "Pharaoh" doesn't let go easily.

Once apartheid was dismantled in South Africa and Nelson Mandela became president, he longed for a new way forward for his people and his nation. Not the old way of revenge and retaliation. He longed for justice not vengeance. Bishop Tutu and others suggested a "Truth and Reconciliation" process. Over the course of several years, perpetrators and victims of heinous crimes faced each other in the presence of mediators and witnesses and listened to each other's stories.

It was an unprecedented effort on a national scale to bring healing to a country ripped by hatred and violence and on the verge of a revengeful bloodbath. It wasn't perfect but it was a small, fitful step in human evolution.

That randomly selected Jew listened to the Nazi's confession in stomach-wrenching detail. When the confession ended, the Jew stood up and left the hospital room *without saying a word.* His silence would forever haunt him. *Did he do the right thing*? That story, Simon Wiesenthal's story, is told in the book, *The Sunflower*. It includes 50 short essays by various people on the question: *What would I have done?*

When someone hurts you or those you love, when you are treated unjustly or cruelly, you have a right to be angry. You have a right to get even. You have a right to seek justice. But you also have the capability, however dim, of forgiving and setting captives free. No, it's not easy. But, in most cases, it's worth it. After all, as someone said, nursing resentments or grudges against someone else is like drinking rat poison and hoping the other person dies. ❧

REFLECTIONS ON A LIFE

Harriet Johnston Arthur: Weaver of Tales

[The following is adapted from a homily presented at the memorial service for Harriet Arthur on Saturday, August 9, 2009. Harriet was known by many in our community and by thousands of tourists to our region. For 15 years she played the role of Barbara Fritchie at the Fritchie House and Museum in Frederick, Maryland.]

For the past several years following memorial services, Harriet would poke me in the chest and say: *So what are you going to say at my service?* And I would always answer: *I don't know. You'll have to wait and see.*

Well, that time has come, and I can now say this about Harriet: She sure could tell a good story. Most of them were true. All of them came with a lesson.

Harriet was a weaver of tales, a teacher of wisdom. She could take sundry and bedraggled threads and weave something beautiful. She could take a sad song and make it better.

Harriet had a *tough* life, as she often told us. But, she would hasten to add, it was a *good* life—punctuated by picnics in Eden, a phrase and an image she treasured to the very end.

Harriet knew that life was hard, sometimes very, very hard. But she knew something else: She knew that grace abounds, which is to say, out of the blue we catch a break time and time again.

Harriet could sure tell a good story. And she didn't mind telling us that her first big story was a big lie. She pretended to be sick in order to stay home from school—she, who would grow up to be a gifted teacher, disliked school from the beginning. She contrived to miss it as often as she could.

Her first lie worked so well she used it again and again until her mother got worried and took her to the hospital. Harriet was thrilled—until the tests came back. To her and her mother's shock and dismay, she had tuberculosis. Harriet was confined to bed for a year. She asked her grandmother what TB was and her grandmother said, "It's like a real bad cold *and then you die.*"

Harriet was terrified and took her "death sentence" to be a punishment from God for lying. That was her notion of God at the time. It concentrated her mind.

So at age 10, with nothing much else to do, young Harriet applied her mind to probing the meaning of death and God. Death, she would conclude, was simply "an incomprehensible mystery." So she'd later say things like: *Don't bother fretting about death. Get on with living. You only live once. Make sure it's enough.*

One of her favorite aphorisms was from Ralph Waldo Emerson. *One of the illusions of life is that the present hour is not the critical, decisive hour. Write it on your heart that every day is the best day in the year.*

The present hour *is* the decisive hour.

At age 10, on what felt like her deathbed, Harriet became a philosopher. She would journey through many churches testing various views of God and suffering until she found peace in a particular Christian tradition that puts God's grace above everything. Life, she would learn, is a sheer gift, a gift to be received with gratitude even if at times we have to grit our teeth.

Harriet's firstborn came into this world severely damaged. At age two, Elizabeth had to be institutionalized. She died at age 18 after a miserable and marginal life.

Harriet never stopped asking why?, why?, why? until, as she put it, an answer of sorts came to her out of the blue. Every life has meaning and purpose; some lives pose tough questions, others seek answers. That consoled her.

In early 1992, Harriet loaded her stroke-stricken husband into her car and drove to Hagerstown where she learned the grim results of a mammogram. On the way home her car overheated. She pulled to the side of the road. It was one of the darkest days of her life. *Here I was*, she said, *with a broken-down car, a broken-down husband, and a broken-down me!*

A stranger stopped and helped arrange for her car to be towed to Bill Trail's service station in Shepherdstown. A few days later a neighbor took her to claim the car. *How much?* she asked Mr. Trail. *Five hundred dollars*, he said. Well, for someone trying to stretch dollars in those tough times, that was a large sum. Nevertheless, she began writing a check. *Don't do that*, said Bill. *You don't have to pay. It's already been paid.*

Harriet was stunned. *Really?! By whom?*

Let's just say, said Bill, *that you have many friends in this town.*

When Harriet told that story, she'd say: *That was the good news. My debt had been paid. The bad news*, she'd say, *was that from then on I had to be nice to everybody in Shepherdstown!*

Well, if I'm not mistaken, that's pretty much the entire Christian gospel in a nutshell: *Your debt's been paid. Get over it. Be kind to everybody!*

Many heard Harriet tell those three stories at one time or another. But not many heard one other story she especially liked. There wasn't much to it as far as stories go—just one sentence—but she mentioned it to me at least twice. It goes like this: On the way out of a certain church one woman remarked to another woman: *But she took communion anyway.*

Harriet was intrigued by that pointed remark—*she took communion anyway*—intrigued by it, in part, because she didn't know what preceded it. *Why was it remarkable for that particular woman to take communion on that particular Sunday?* Apparently, against conventional standards of piety *that woman* had claimed the grace offered through Christ in broken bread and crushed grape. I don't know why that remark made a lasting impression on Harriet, but I'm guessing it's because *that particular woman* represented both a *bodacious defiance and a tender humility* before the Holy.

Over many, many years, Sunday after Sunday after Sunday, Harriet sat there on the second pew, musing on the gospel story, that story of amazing grace that transforms hateful sinners into loving sinners, greedy sinners into generous sinners, and embittered sinners into glad and joyful sinners. Time and time again she brought her broken body and soul to the community Table to partake of the mysterious presence of Christ, which is to say, the mysterious presence of Love. And time after time I could almost hear her whispering: *But she took communion anyway.*

Now and then a woman like Harriet walks into our lives and we see what grace and graciousness can do. Yes, life is hard, sometimes very, very hard. But grace abounds time and time again. ❧

JEWS AND CHRISTIANS

The Third Word From the Cross

Holy Week will soon be here. On Good Friday churches around the world will recite and reflect upon "The Seven Last Words of Christ" from the cross. *Father, forgive them for they know not what they do. Today you will be with me in paradise. Women, behold your son; son, behold your mother. I thirst. Why have you forsaken me? It is finished. Into your hands I commend my spirit.*

The Third Word is: *Woman, behold your son; son, behold your mother.*

Meanwhile, standing near the cross were his mother, and his mother's sister, Mary the wife of Clopas, and Mary Magdalene. When Jesus saw his mother and the disciple whom he loved standing beside her, he said to his mother, 'Woman, here is your son.' Then he said to the disciple, 'Here is your mother.' And from that hour the disciple took her into his own home. (John 19:26–27)

Jesus couldn't move his hands. He could barely move his head, but he could move his eyes. He looked at his mother then toward his disciple and said, *'Woman, here is your son.'* And then looking back toward his mother, *'Here is your mother.'* And from that hour the disciple took her into his own home.

That disciple took the mother of Jesus home, beat her up and pushed her out into the cold, dark night where she and her children were bound, gagged, and dragged away to ghettos and gas chambers.

I know, I know, it doesn't say that in the gospel pages. But that's what happened. Not to Mary herself but to her people. Beat up and pushed out into the cold, dark night. Bound, gagged, and dragged away to ghettos and gas chambers.

In this gospel, replete with symbolism, Mary, we might say, represents "Judaism"; and the beloved disciple, we might say, represents the fledgling community that arose in the wake of Jesus' death and eventually became known as "the Church."

It will do us good on any day, but especially on Good Friday, to remember how Christians turned Jews into scapegoats and crucified them in more ways than one, in more places than one, in more centuries than one.

Jesus said to his mother, *'Woman, here is your son.' And to his disciple, 'Here is your mother.'* With his dying breath Jesus was trying to create a new kind of community, formed by love and not by family or tribal blood.

Judaism gave birth to Mary. Mary gave birth to Jesus. And Jesus gave birth to a new community, to a new way of being and living in this world, a way that transcends tribal divisions of one kind and another. It's the right way, but it's not an easy way.

It's hard to be true and faithful in this world. So much can go wrong in the best of persons and communities. Much has gone wrong in the Church. Without God's grace and forgiveness none of us stands a chance.

It will do the Church good to remember how Christians turned Jews into scapegoats and crucified them in more ways than one. It will do the Church good to remember and to repent. Now as bad as the news is, there is also good news: There is more grace in God than sin in us.

On what would eventually be called Good Friday, while he bled on the cross, Jesus said: *'Woman, here is your son.' And to his disciple, 'Here is your mother.'*

But Christians would turn Good Friday into a rally day and terrorize the Jewish people for 2,000 years. It's not what Jesus had in mind. He didn't have another religion in mind, least of all one that would become sectarian, exclusive, and bellicose. That's not what Jesus held in his heart.

You can hear the heart of Jesus elsewhere in this gospel. *For God so loved the world.* God so loved the world. Not the Jewish world or the Christian world or the Muslim world or the Buddhist world or the Hindu world or the Sikh, Jain, or Baha'i worlds, or the humanist, animist, or atheist worlds. God so loved the *world*. The *whole* world. Period.

Jesus never meant for his way to become a way of exclusion and terrorism. *I am the way, the truth, and the life* meant *love* is the way. He didn't mean that Christianity was the way to heaven and all other religions were not. He didn't mean that he was the way to another place at all. He meant that love is the way to live here and now.

Those who abide in love abide in God, he said. *I am in the Father and the Father is in me. I am in you and you are in me. God is love and those who abide in love abide in God. Come and see where I abide,* he said. *In my Father's house are many mansions, many rooms, many dwelling places, not just one.* In other words, there are many ways to dwell in God, which is to say, to dwell in love.

It will do the Church good to remember how Christians turned against Jews, the very people of our Lord's mother. But remembering is not enough. The Church must also repent and make amends.

It's hard to believe but it's true: Only in the past 50 years or so has the Church begun to acknowledge and appreciate a simple fact: *Jesus was not a Christian.* Jesus was Jewish, a child of a Jewish mother and father, who themselves were children of Abraham and Sarah, who long, long ago found and then nursed a promise in their hearts, a promise that someday their children and their children's children would find a way to bless all the families, tribes, and nations of the whole earth—a way of love, not a way of hate; a way of mercy, not a way of torture; a way of forgiveness, not a way of revenge; a way of inclusion not a way of exclusion.

Jesus didn't invent that promise. He embraced the promise. And then nursed and cultivated it in his heart.

It's an ancient, precious, and fragile promise, blessed, broken open, and given each time Christians gather round the Table of Our Lord. *By this will all people know you are my disciples, if you love one another.* There is no other way. For Christians or anyone else. Love is the way.

Here is a verse from the traditional "Solemn Reproaches of the Cross," often read in churches on Good Friday:

O my people, O my Church,
What have I done to you,
or in what have I offended you?
Answer me.
I grafted you into the tree of my chosen Israel,
and you turned on them with persecution and mass murder.
I made you joint heirs with them of my covenants
but you made them scapegoats for your own guilt,
and you have prepared a cross for your Savior.
Lord, have mercy.

And God is. Merciful. Good Friday is a good day to remember that God is merciful. And if God is, shall we not also be? ❧

SUMMER 2010

REASONS FOR HOPE

Oil is pouring into the Gulf of Mexico. It's a growing catastrophe with no end in sight. Are there reasons for hope? I think so. It may be a stretch but one reason is this affirmation from the Apostle Paul.

Suffering produces endurance, and endurance produces character, and character produces hope, and hope does not disappoint, because God's love has been poured into our hearts through the Holy Spirit. (Romans 5:35)

Here in this county and all around the world people are in a state of shock at the sight of oil gushing into the waters we know as the Gulf of Mexico. All around the world people weep for dying fish, birds, plants, and habitats. All around the world people lament their own complicity in a bloated, carefree lifestyle that requires reckless exploitation of the earth and her creatures. Here and around the world people are indignant and screaming for change. And that's reason for hope.

Not all people in all places, to be sure, but enough people in enough places to give us reasons for hope.

The Maker's own love for the earth has been poured into our hearts.

Engineers, mechanics, and biologists are working furiously not just for money, though some might, but because they love this earth and are bound and determined to mend this catastrophic wound. They have not given up. And that's reason for hope.

Federal, state, and local government officials are working furiously not just for reelection, though some might, but because they love this earth and are bound and determined to mend this catastrophic wound. And that's reason for hope.

Louisiana fishermen, shrimp trawlers, environmentalists, fish and game wardens, and countless ordinary citizens are working furiously, dabbing oil from the wings of brown pelicans not for money or praise, but because they love this earth and are bound and determined to mend this catastrophic wound. They have not given up. And that's reason for hope.

Hope is hard work.

Do not think that you or we alone seethe and weep, or that we alone love and care for the earth and its creatures, or that we are the first to appreciate the earth's wonder and fragility, or our own godlike potential for good and ill. Millions upon millions of people do and have for a long, long time.

Listen to this anthem composed nearly 3,000 years ago by a poet in the Jewish tradition.

> *O LORD, our Sovereign, how majestic is your name in all the earth! You have set your glory above the heavens. When I look at your heavens, the work of your fingers, the moon and the stars that you have established; what are human beings that you are mindful of them, mortals that you care for them? Yet you have made them a little lower than God, and crowned them with glory and honor. You have given them dominion over the works of your hands; you have put all things under their feet, all sheep and oxen, and also the beasts of the field, the birds of the air, and the fish of the sea, whatever passes along the paths of the seas. O LORD, our Sovereign, how majestic is your name in all the earth!* (Psalm 8)

Of course, we don't need the Bible or a special revelation to tell us the earth is majestic or to tell us that we humans among all the species on earth possess divinelike powers to create and destroy, or that we of all creatures have self-consciousness and, with it, responsibility like none other. Whether it's been "given" or not, we have *assumed* dominion, which is to say, a governing responsibility that makes us accountable *for* and *to* other creatures, not to mention our accountability to the Maker of heaven and earth.

We are moral creatures. And that's why we feel guilty, or should, when we mess up, and why we blame ourselves, or somebody, *anybody*! We are *responsible* creatures and at our best we know it.

Sin and immorality have consequences. We know there are things that *ought not to be done* but are; and we know there are things that *ought to be done* but aren't. We are moral creatures. Pity the person, agency, or company that feels no guilt.

It's true: Guilt and judgment can paralyze and polarize us. But, in proper doses, guilt and judgment can lead to repentance and modification of attitudes and behavior. And time and time again they have. Judgment often precedes grace. And that's reason for hope.

All around the world people lamented the devastation of Haiti in the wake of the earthquake. And sure enough, people arose as one to bring salvation and redemption to the Haitian people. We now possess tools for instant global communication. And that's reason for hope.

All around the world people lament the economic destruction inflicted by reckless financial institutions on innocent people and families. We are learning again that there's enough for everyone's need but not for everyone's greed, enough for livelihoods, not enough for lifestyles. We keep learning and relearning. And that's reason for hope.

All around the world, like never before, people are condemning wars that fatten the coffers of warlords and military industrial machines while destroying lives and nations and what human hands took years to build. People are repenting of ancient animosities and pledging to work for peace and justice. And that's reason for hope.

All around the world people lament contaminated water, contaminated food, and the inhumane treatment of animals. We are once again growing safer, healthier food closer to home. The Shepherdstown Farmers Market is an example. And that's reason for hope.

In this moment things may look hopeless. But consider this possibility: the universe arose out of love, as a sheer gift, not out of chance or necessity.

Love throbs in every atom, every molecule, and every vein. The earth is good and that goodness includes us, its most complex and wayward children.

Yes, we mess up, time and time again. There's no use pretending we don't.

But, still, the continual presence of grace leads repentant and humble souls back to their senses when they go astray. The spirit at work in this awesomely beautiful world for 4.5 billion years is the same spirit in humanity. The heart and face of that evolving spirit some would say is Christ, "The Anointed," or the Beloved, the First Word, not unlike the Tao, Logos, Wisdom, Atman, and the Great Spirit in other traditions.

The First Word, which is to say, Love, was present 15 or so billion years ago in the first burst of light, in the first moment of time and space, wending its way through atoms, minerals, molecules, stars and galaxies; wending its way through earth's soupy waters, seaweed, starfish, grasses, trees, animals and into humanity, playfully calling and nudging all things to greater and greater complexity, greater and greater freedom and awareness. Over eons of time "the Beloved" has been arising in and through it all, blessing all things and all matter of things all along the evolutionary path.

Nothing in heaven or earth can destroy that love. It keeps rising out of death, going ahead of us, preparing even more communion and greater community to come. We have been loved into being over a long, long time.

Yes, we are tempted to resist and refuse love. And, yes, we are tempted to resign in despair and give up. But we mustn't.

Hope is hard work.

None of us can save or redeem the whole world. But we can do good and holy work in the world close at hand, inch by inch, marsh by marsh, bird by bird, person by person, community by community.

Once upon a time a little girl came upon a beach covered with starfish. Starfish had washed ashore by the thousands and were slowly dying in the sun. She stood frozen in shock. Tears filled her eyes. Then she stooped and picked up a starfish and flung it back into the sea, and then another and another, furiously working her way down the long beach.

An old man watched at a distance and called out to her. *Little, girl,* he said. *Don't bother. It doesn't matter. There are way too many.*

The girl stopped and looked at the man. Then she reached down and picked up another starfish and flung it back into the sea. And then turning toward the man she pointed out to the sea and said: *It matters to that one.*

We have assumed dominion. Now what? ❧

BUILDING ON SACRED GROUND

A week or so ago I had my eyes fixed on a gospel story about Jesus healing a crippled woman on the Sabbath, but my concentration was continually interrupted by shrill voices protesting the building of a mosque near Ground Zero, *ground* which many people consider sacred the way the ruler of the synagogue in the gospel story considered the Sabbath to be sacred *time*.

The guardians of the Sabbath wanted to protect sacred time from inappropriate infringement. And to me that sounded a bit like the squabble around the proposed Islamic community center in New York City.

Look, the guardians of the Sabbath said to Jesus, *we don't mind if you heal this woman; just don't do it on the Sabbath. You're more than welcome to heal her, but do it on some other day, a couple blocks from today. After all, we have very strong feelings about the Sabbath. It's holy.*

To all of which Jesus basically said, *You're right. The Sabbath is holy. What a great time to set a woman free from her crippling bondage.*

And the Sabbath was the perfect day to set a body free from bondage *unless you'd forgotten what made the Sabbath holy in the first place.* And, as it turns out, Ground Zero is the perfect spot for building a mosque *unless we've forgotten what makes America holy ground in the first place.* There's a lot more to the holiness of American soil than Ground Zero.

Anyway, here's the gospel story I had my eyes on:

> *On a Sabbath Jesus was teaching in one of the synagogues. A woman was there who had been crippled by a spirit for 18 years. She was bent over and could not straighten up at all. When Jesus saw her, he called her forward. "Woman, you are set free from your infirmity." Then he put his hands on her, and immediately she straightened up and praised God.*
>
> *Indignant—because Jesus had healed on the Sabbath—the synagogue ruler said to the people, "There are six days for work. Come and be healed on those days, not on the Sabbath."*
>
> *Jesus answered, "You hypocrites! Doesn't each of you on the Sabbath untie his ox or donkey from the stall and lead it out to give it water? So, then, should not this woman, a daughter of Abraham, whom Satan has kept bound for 18 long years, be set free on the Sabbath day from what bound her?"*
>
> *When he said this, all his opponents were humiliated, but the people were delighted.* (Luke 13:10–17)

Leaders in both political parties oppose the "mosque" and leaders in both parties support it. Some Muslims are for it; some against it. The families of the 9/11 victims are divided. Some for; some against.

In one sense it's none of our business. It's for New Yorkers to decide. But in another sense it is our business because it raises the question of what is *truly holy* about America.

First a few facts. The so-called Ground Zero mosque is actually two blocks from Ground Zero but close enough in the minds of many to contaminate the holiness of the site. It's actually a *community center* not a mosque per se. It will have a swimming pool, basketball court, and museum honoring victims of 9/11, some of whom, in case you hadn't heard, were American Muslims. But the proposed building is not just any center. It is an *Islamic* community center and for many: "Say no more."

The center's imam, Mr. Abdul Rauf, is of the *Sufi* branch of Islam, a form of Islam that is open, tolerant, peaceful, and pluralistic. Osama bin Laden and al-Qaida hate Rauf-type Muslims, which should make us glad to call him our ally. You'd think so. But *feelings* often undermine *thinking*, which, by the way, is why we are governed by a constitution and not the whims and tantrums of a monarch or the whims and tantrums of popular opinion. We can and should be so very grateful for the Constitution, which keeps our temperamental feelings in check.

And finally from the list of facts: The attacks on the Twin Towers and the Pentagon were executed by 19 *criminals*—please, don't honor them as *warriors*!—blinded by an extremely perverted form of Islam not unlike others who have slaughtered thousands in the name of Christ and under the sign of the cross. *Please*, Christians say, *don't paint all Christians with that brush.*

Apparently many Americans aren't willing to see differences within Islam, a historic religious tradition as diverse as Christianity. Do we consider *all born-again Christians* "abortion doctor murderers" because one was? Do we consider *all Orthodox Christians* "mass murderers" because the Serbian warlord Milosevic and his henchmen were? Do we consider *all Catholics* "terrorists" because, well, don't you know about those bombings in Northern Ireland?

Actually, Catholics were suspect in this country from the beginning. Their loyalty to America was questioned during the French and American War. In fact, if it hadn't been for a few outspoken Quakers, Catholics would not have been permitted to build a church in Philadelphia, the "City of Brotherly Love." Catholics were considered alien, unclean, dangerous, "other" as were Jews and Mormons in other times and places—as are Muslims now.

You are unfit, say some Americans. *You are unfit and unworthy to stand or kneel near our holy ground.*

And thus we shackle the souls of American Muslims with indignities as surely as "Satan" bound the woman in the gospel story. *Don't you dare stand up and look us in the eye as equals.*

Any day but the Sabbath, screeched the guardians of the Sabbath. *The Sabbath is holy.*

To which Jesus said: *What better day*? For Jesus, you see, remembered the origins and spirit of the Sabbath. Do you?

More than a thousand years before Jesus, his people had been slaves in Egypt. They were worked like mules. Day after day after day, one day just like the next, working like mules for hundreds of years.

But once Moses led them out of bondage he quickly instituted the Sabbath Day. One day in seven would be free of toil. It was a time to remember what it meant to be "human." It was a time to be fully human, alive, joyful, and free of burdens. Moses—the Great Liberator in more ways than one—was determined to protect that day as *holy* lest his people turn themselves back into slaves of work. One day in seven to unplug, breathe, jump for joy. The Sabbath. Liberation and rest.

Guess what happened to that good idea? The spirit of the day was corrupted and crushed by rules and regulations. The one day devoted to release from bondage became itself an onerous burden. It was still called "holy," but it wasn't.

Yes, Jesus could have waited until Monday or Tuesday. But he was looking for more than just *one* healing. He was looking to heal his people by calling them back to the Sabbath's true holiness.

Have Americans forgotten what makes this land truly holy? It's not the innocence or purity of its people. It's not the blood that has been shed at Antietam or Ground Zero. What makes America holy is a radical idea, a conviction inscribed in our Declaration of Independence: *All people are created equal and endowed by their Creator with certain inalienable rights.*

And that's not all. There's also this revolutionary conviction in the First Amendment: *Congress shall make no law respecting an establishment of religion, or prohibiting the free exercise thereof; or abridging the freedom of speech.*

So, yes, of course, a mosque should be built *right at Ground Zero* in order to show the world *what is truly holy about America.* That site may be hallowed. But there's something even more hallowed about America. It's the dream that proclaims all people equal and with the inalienable right to worship freely and in safety.

In case you've forgotten: We were all outsiders at one time. We are all lucky to have been accepted into this beautiful country. Protestants came to this country in the first place because they were unwelcome in their homelands. And should we not be the first to welcome Muslims who are not only children of Abraham like us but also children of God? ❧

PEACE ON EARTH

The Jesus or Nike Way

Christmas choirs will hail Jesus as King of Kings and Lord of Lords. But to tell you the truth, Christians should be a little reluctant to sing along, since in that name wars have been waged and peoples subjugated. In the 4th century, Emperor Constantine established the precedent by emblazoning crosses on Roman shields. And soon thereafter Christendom was established—by the sword—all across Europe.

Christendom was not the kind of kingdom Jesus envisioned. Christ was not that kind of king.

Consequently many of us are as reluctant to call Christ "king" today as Jesus was reluctant to be called "Christ" in his day. Let me explain.

First, Christ is a title, not a last name. Jesus was not the son of Mr. and Mrs. Christ. I know, I know, most of us know that, but it doesn't hurt to review basics.

Christos is the Greek word for the Hebrew word *Messiah,* which means "anointed." It can refer to a king, prophet, or priest anointed to serve the people.

For several hundred years before Jesus, the title Messiah was widely and somewhat loosely used. But eventually it came to symbolize a singular Jewish hope for someone anointed by the Spirit of God who would save them from their oppressors and redeem their broken spirits, *the way we hope someone or something will save our country from moral and economic bankruptcy without our having to change our ways.*

Wouldn't that be nice? Yeah boy, I'd vote for *that* Messiah! For hundreds of years, the Jewish people had suffered under the heels of occupying forces: the Babylonians, the Greeks and, finally the Romans. Humiliation bred resentment and insurgencies, *not unlike what we have seen in Iraq and Afghanistan.*

Imagine, if you can, the forces of a foreign country occupying American cities and taking anything and everything they wanted. How long would it take an insurgency to arise in our country?

How long, O Lord, how long? O come, O come, Emmanuel and ransom captive Israel.

Some people wait for the Lord. Others take things into their own hands. Under the Roman occupation, certain zealots had claimed the title Messiah in order to inspire an insurgency. The Romans squashed them all.

Jesus himself dismissed that title in part because of its nationalistic and militaristic overtones. Jesus, as it turns out, was brewing a different kind of spirit.

At that time it was commonly believed that the Messiah would be a warrior king like David, who, you may remember, slew the Philistines like so many stink bugs. Jesus wanted no part of that messianic complex.

It's true, the image of the Messiah sprouted in Jewish soil, but in time it would become something else. The image of Christ would transmute into a symbol of universal love—at least for a while. You can see evidence of its evolution in certain first-century letters.

And now to the "Jesus" part of Jesus Christ.

The name *Jesus* (or, Jesu) is the Aramaic equivalent of *Joshua*, the warlord who succeeded Moses and succeeded in conquering Palestine after appointing 12 mighty swordsmen, one from each tribe, to plan and execute a bloody military invasion. According to the book of Joshua, those 12 tribes splashed across the Jordan River, slaughtered many of the native inhabitants and hijacked their lands and houses, *not unlike certain European Christians who splashed across the Delaware and Mississippi, killing Indians and hijacking their lands.*

As you can see, when you're God's *chosen* people, when you're *exceptional*, when you've been given a *destiny*, other people better get out of your way. That's one image of God. But it's not the image that Jesus offered. The God Jesus reveals is crucified with the victims of the Roman Empire. *And that kind of God is hard to imagine.*

In Joshua's day, the human mind and heart were stuck on tribalism, a form of "survival of the fittest." The human heart was stuck and would not budge. But something was stirring within the earth and within the human heart and brain that would not be denied.

It shows up in the gospels. The name *Jesus* is the Aramaic equivalent of *Joshua*. Why is that important? It's important as background for seeing the story of Jesus unfold.

According to the gospels, Jesus, like Joshua, also splashed in the River Jordan and then very deliberately appointed 12 men—but not *swords*men. Jesus appointed a motley company including several smelly fishermen, a reviled tax collector, a zealot, and a starry-eyed poet. With these 12 in tow, plus other men and women, Jesus "invaded" the same land Joshua had invaded.

But Jesus' hand held no sword. His hands healed the sick, fed the hungry, and lifted up the fallen. He proclaimed and embodied a new day, a kingdom (kin-dom) of love and justice meant for this earth. "Thy kingdom come on earth."

The contrast between Jesus and Joshua was very clear to those who first conveyed the gospel of Christ's kingdom, as was the contrast with the Roman kingdom. Caesar Augustus, just like Joshua, wanted to save his own people and usher in world peace (Pax Romana) *just like the United States wants to save its people and usher in world peace.* Joshua and Caesar saved their people and worked for peace by destroying those who stood in their way. Their way to world peace would be through violence.

It's the ancient myth of redemptive violence.

Kill the bad people and all will be well. Peace through victory (or Nike, the Roman god of victory).

Joshua, which means "savior," saved his people and their way of life by violence. Jesus, which also means savior, saved his people by loving his enemies even if it killed him. He made peace by the blood of his cross, *not by the blood of his enemies.*

Those who joined his movement would also work for peace by way of healing and restorative justice. As it turns out, nothing in heaven or earth, and certainly nothing in Rome, could keep that kind of love down.

And so when *that* Jesus and *all that love* rose out of the grave, Jesus would be declared King of Kings, Lord of Lord, Son of God, which was a way of saying to the world that Jesus and this way of love were more powerful than the Roman emperor, whose image was displayed across the world, *the way the United States' "image" is displayed by hundreds of military bases all around the world.* In both cases the message is clear: submit or else.

In the first century the image of Caesar Augustus was displayed throughout the world with these titles: King of King, Lord of Lords, Prince of Peace, Son of God. Thus, in the first century, there was a clash of images and myths. It was a question of loyalty and allegiance. Who will you give your heart to? Who or what will save you? Whose kingdom will you serve?

That was the question in the first century. And it's the question before us today. Peace through military victory or peace through restorative justice?

In Christ all the fullness of God was pleased to dwell, and through him God was pleased to reconcile to himself all things, whether on earth or in heaven, by making peace through the blood of his cross. (From a first-century letter written to a fledgling group in the Roman city of Colossi.) Just when you think this is only about Jesus, it turns out to be about each of us. The fullness of God is pleased to dwell in human flesh, pleased to dwell in humanity. The fullness of God, which is to say Love, is pleased to dwell in each of us. And it's just dying to come alive. ❧

SPRING 2011

BLESSED FOOLS

Blessed are the poor in spirit,
for theirs is the kingdom of heaven.
Blessed are the meek,
for they shall inherit the earth.
Blessed are the pure in heart,
for they will see God.
— The Beatitudes

If you're going to follow the way of Jesus, let's face it, you've got to be a little crazy. You've got to live upside down in this world. All reasonable people know "the meek" are not going to "inherit the earth." Not in our lifetime. Forget it.

It's possible Jesus offered all those "rewards" with a wink and a nod. *Yeah, right,* he might have said. *That ain't gonna happen—unless you're crazy enough to believe it.*

The same goes for "the pure in heart." All reasonable people know the pure in heart will not "see God," because no one does. The Bible itself plainly says so elsewhere.

Let's face it, if you're going to follow the way of Jesus you've got to be a little crazy. You've got to live upside down—without a safety net.

All reasonable people know that "those who hunger and thirst for righteousness and justice" will never be "satisfied." Not in our lifetime. Justice is perpetually elusive. You might as well try to catch the wind.

If you're going to follow Jesus you've got to be a little crazy because there are no tangible rewards. Not here anyway.

"Blessed are you when people revile you and persecute you and utter all kinds of evil against you falsely *on my account*. Rejoice and be glad, for your reward is great in heaven, for in the same way they persecuted the prophets who were before you." (Matthew 5:11–12)

Yeah, right, we say. *That's exactly what I want. I want to be reviled, ridiculed, and persecuted in this life so I can get a reward—* yet to be named!*—in the next life. What do you take me for? A fool?*

Apparently, Jesus was happy to take in fools, for he knew that fools might actually live the radical way of love. As it turns out, in these Lessons on the Mount Jesus was constituting a movement of "blessed fools" who might, who just might transform the world.

For example, in the Jesus movement, the "end" would not justify any and all "means." Peace would not come by killing all the bad people in the world. Yes, empires keep trying to kill their way to world peace but it just doesn't work. There is another way.

Blessed are the peacemakers, Jesus says. Blessed are those who get in between violent factions. Blessed are those who get in the way of violence.

If you're going to follow Jesus, you've got to be a little crazy. You've got to love your enemy even if it kills you, which is why the Apostle Paul admitted in 1 Corinthians 1:18 that the cross is foolishness from the perspective of reason and common sense: *For the message about the cross is foolishness to those who are perishing, but to us who are being saved it is the power of God—* which is to say, the power of Love.

If you're going to follow Jesus, you've got to be a little crazy.

For example, when a snobbish superior smacks your cheek with the back of her hand, you bite your tongue and turn the other cheek, forcing her to smack you with an open palm, which, ironically, in Jesus' time and place would have shown respect for your dignity. That bit of clownish wisdom comes later in the Lessons on the Mount, after Jesus has first honored holy foolishness. (The Beatitudes)

If someone strikes you on the cheek, turn the other cheek, said Jesus.

What do you take me for? A fool?

Apparently, Jesus was happy to take in fools, for he knew that fools might actually practice the radical way of love in a way that overly reasonable people can't or won't.

For example, when a soldier of the hated occupying army forces you to carry his pack a mile, insist on carrying it two just to show him you're not a compliant victim and which, by the way, also makes him look bad in the eyes of his commander. That bit of clownish wisdom also comes later in the Lesson on the Mount, after Jesus has first honored holy foolishness.

Nonviolence, you see, isn't *passivity* in the face of evil. It's creative resistance to evil. Think Gandhi; think Martin Luther King. Nonviolent resistance requires imagination and courage. Violence is the childish way. Even certain decorated U.S. military leaders have finally seen the light.

When I became an adult, says the Apostle Paul, *I put away childish things and took up the way of Love. Love is patient. Love is kind. Love does not insist on its own way.* (1 Corinthians 13)

If you're forced to walk a mile, said Jesus, walk two. If someone demands your coat give him your underwear too, and just walk away.

See what I mean? If you're going to follow Jesus you've got to be a little crazy. But, take heart: You'll be in good company, for there is a long line of honored Christians called "Holy Fools" or "Fools for Christ."

St. Francis is ranked high among the blessed fools. Francis gave away trunks and trunks of his fine clothing to the poor and then walked out of town naked, following the call of Christ to be a servant of love.

St. Francis was a blessed fool as was Xenia, the 19th-century Russian Orthodox widow who wore rags while distributing her husband's military pension to the poor. She was reviled, mocked, and beaten, but following her death she was declared a saint—a blessed fool.

There's actually a website listing famous Holy Fools for Christ, including the first one, Simeon of Syria, a sixth-century hermit. Simeon is considered the patron saint of holy fools and the patron saint of *puppeteers*—which, I suppose, only goes to prove the point.

No, you don't have to mimic their behavior. That would be on the *stupid* side of foolish. But you can cultivate their blessed outlook on the world.

Blessed are the poor, says Jesus to the assembled crowd. And, I suspect, he said it with a twinkle in his eye because he knew what everybody knows: People want to be rich, not poor. Blessed are those who mourn, he says, knowing full well that people want to be happy not sad. Blessed are the meek even though pushy people seem to get their way in this world.

Surely Jesus knew the meek are not going to inherit the earth. But he says it anyway because he's building a community of blessed fools who are just too foolish to even care about rewards.

Here's how the Apostle Paul put it:

> *God chose what is foolish in the world to shame the wise; God chose what is weak in the world to shame the strong; God chose what is low and despised in the world, things that are not, to reduce to nothing things that are, so that no one might boast in the presence of God.* (1 Corinthians 1:27–29)

If you're going to follow the way of Jesus, let's face it, you've got to be a little crazy.

For example, you walk away from your successful fishing business in order to learn from a homeless rabbi how to "fish for people," which sounds very, very fishy but you do it anyway because…well, you don't know why and probably never will. *Come, walk with me, says the Spirit, and I will show you a way to draw people out of the sea of misery.* Maybe that's what Jesus meant.

Anyway, Peter, Andrew, James, and John took the lure. And the next thing they saw was a swarm of people coming their way. (Matthew 4:18–25) The sea of humanity poured in around Jesus' feet—more than anyone could count or fathom. So Jesus withdrew up the mountain and there he described the kind of people who would be salt of the earth and light of the world.

It wouldn't be the greedy and smug. It would be the poor and lowly.

It wouldn't be the vengeful. It would be the merciful.

It wouldn't be people armed with swords. It would be people armed with bread, medicine, shovels, books, and poetry.

It wouldn't be people basking in arrogance and exceptionalism. It would be people basking in a blessing that no one or nothing can ever take away.

You see, in the end, we are not called to be consumers or even producers. We are called to be people who bless the world—to love, to forgive, to hope— especially when hate seems all around. And if that's foolish, so be it. ❧

SUMMER 2011

THE FLAG AND SENATOR BYRD

In honor of Senator Robert Byrd on the first anniversary of his death.
(November 20, 1917–June 28, 2010)

July Fourth will soon be here. American flags will wave all across the nation. Flags will hang from poles, windows, bridges, and cranes. Flags will hang in many churches—but not in all. And for good reasons.

Even though Americans love the flag and the republic for which it stands, we can love something more. We can love the vision and possibility of "the peaceable kingdom," the world and all its people and nations as one family.

Yes, we love our country and its flag, as we love our parents, grandparents, children, and grandchildren. But we must not worship our children, parents, or country. And therein lies a tricky trap.

Thirteen years ago, on Friday, September 11, 1998, in one of the biggest surprises of my life, Senator Robert C. Byrd invited me to sit with him on the sofa in his office. He wanted to hear my views on the proposed constitutional amendment that would make burning or desecrating the flag a criminal offense. The so-called flag-burning amendment was coming before Congress *yet again*.

On the surface the amendment sounds patriotic, but it actually undermines one of our greatest freedoms: freedom of speech, including dissent against the government. Most senators do not want such an amendment to the Constitution, but they are afraid to vote against it. Imagine what an opponent could do in a televised sound bite with a vote *against* "protecting the American flag."

In 1998 Senator Byrd was considered the "swing vote" on this amendment, and for the first time he was leaning toward supporting it, in part, because so many ministers in West Virginia had urged him to vote for it in the name of "God and country." The American Civil Liberties Union contacted me to provide the senator with "an alternative Christian perspective." Tom Moses and Dave Ricks, two decorated veterans of World War II, had volunteered to go as well.

Tom and Dave strongly opposed the amendment. They had fought and risked their lives, they said, to protect our freedoms, including the right to burn our country's flag. We met with Byrd's staff for an hour and then were invited to meet the senator himself, something we had not expected.

As we entered the senator's main office, he was just leaving. But once he learned that we were *West Virginians*, and two World War II veterans at that, he stopped in his tracks and ordered his photographer to take a picture of us with him.

Tom and Dave quickly stepped up beside the senator. I held my ground. The senator motioned for me to get in the picture. I declined. My refusal disturbed the senator—and it showed.

Why won't you get in this picture?

With all due respect, Senator, I am a minister of the church and not your chaplain.

I had in mind Billy Graham and how he had compromised his ministry and integrity by appearing too chummy with Nixon and other presidents. Not that I'm Billy Graham or that Byrd was Nixon. Not even close! But you get the idea.

Anyway, my refusal really peeved Senator Byrd. *Look,* he said, *I don't care if you are a minister. You are one of my constituents and I want you in this picture.* At that point I realized this was making a scene totally unrelated to the purpose of our visit. So I relented and got in the picture.

Well, as it turned out, my brief resistance aroused the senator's curiosity. Although he was late for a meeting, he asked us to sit down and explain our views. When my turn came I acknowledged the senator's deep respect for the Constitution, the flag, and the Bible. I mentioned that if burning a flag *desecrated* it, then somehow it had been made *sacred*. And since the second commandment forbids us to make idols of anything, we probably shouldn't turn the flag into one.

The senator was quiet for a few moments and then said: *I never thought of it that way.* Then he thanked us for coming and left for his meeting.

When the vote was taken that fall, Senator Byrd once again stood his ground against the silly amendment. To be sure, he had more than one reason to vote against it.

I have long admired Senator Byrd. I admired his wisdom and courage; even more, I admired his willingness to grow in humility and grace over the years, his willingness to admit his wrongs publicly, and to ask for forgiveness. And, above all, I admired him for putting his love of God above his love of country.

Many years ago, Christ called Senator Byrd to walk the hard path of love, to keep growing and growing in love. It's not enough to love self, family, tribe, or nation. We are called to love all people, including our enemies, because God is love and all people are God's children.

And that's why many churches do not display a flag. A flag in church has tempted many a citizen—from Spain to England, from Germany to our own country—to put nation above or beside God. It's not God *and* country. It's country *under* God as our Pledge of Allegiance puts it.

We are not a Christian nation and for that we should be glad. The wall of separation between church and state fixed in our Constitution is one of the most brilliant convictions of the Founding Fathers—perhaps *the* most brilliant. As the church in Nazi Germany discovered to its everlasting regret and shame, *patriotism joined with religion is a powerful and often deadly combination.*

As Americans we love our country. But Christians, especially those who follow Jesus, must be vigilant lest they give unconditional allegiance to anything less than God.

We hold these truths to be self-evident, that all men are created equal, that they are endowed by their Creator with certain inalienable Rights, that among these are Life, Liberty and the pursuit of Happiness.

All *men* are created equal.

The founders—like all inspired poets and prophets—said more than they meant. They might have meant *men* in a narrow sense, but the spirit of that document meant *women,* too. They might have meant *white people,* but the spirit of that document meant *people of color,* too. They might have meant *Americans only,* but the spirit of that document meant *all people of every tribe and nation.*

The founders of this nation unwittingly resurrected the ancient vision of the peaceable kingdom—the world as a community of goods shared in communion with all peoples, tribes, and nations. No wonder the Declaration of Independence has been a beacon of hope to the world. And that makes me so very, very proud to be an American.

We hold these truths to be self-evident, that all people in all nations are created equal, that they are endowed by their Creator with certain inalienable Rights.

That faith and that conviction continue to haunt and inspire, to judge and inform our nation's domestic and foreign policies. Yes, the world of politics is complicated and messy, but let us never, ever tire of working on and for the bold dream that called our nation into being. ❧

FALL 2011

THE NEWS TODAY

Taking the five loaves and the two fish, Jesus looked up to heaven, and blessed and broke the loaves, and gave them to the disciples, and the disciples gave them to the crowds.
— MATTHEW 14:13–21

I read the news today, oh boy, about a lucky man who made the grade. And if you know this song by the Beatles, you know things didn't turn out so well for that lucky man who made the grade. But by the time "A Day in the Life" is over *we know how many holes it takes to fill the Albert Hall.* Which remains a riddle for the ages.

I read the news today, oh boy, about a lucky nation that made the grade, and if you know this story, you know things aren't turning out so well for the lucky nation that made the grade, then lost its way and got a downgrade. Now, I guess, we know how many holes it takes to fill the House, the Senate, and the White House, too. Which is a riddle of a different sort.

I read the news today and yesterday and every day last week and the week before and, oh boy, it doesn't look so good for this nation or the world. It's downright depressing, which may be why some people don't read the news or watch it.

I read the news today, oh boy. The stock market plunged. Again. Another trillion dollars lost.

I read the news today, oh boy. Famine in Africa. Again. Another thousand children dead in Somalia.

I read the news today, oh boy. A bloody massacre in Norway. Seventy youth executed in cold blood by a so-called Christian crusader enraged by the so-called Muslim colonization of so-called Christian European soil.

I read the news today, oh boy. Deadly mudslides in South Korea, a train wreck in China, predatory priests in Ireland, bankruptcy in Greece, brutal crackdowns in Syria, suicide bombs in Iraq, civilians bombed in Afghanistan, nuclear weapons in Iran, an earthquake in Haiti, a drought in Texas, a tsunami in Japan....or was that yesterday?!

I read the news today, oh boy. Ten years after 9/11 we've killed a hundredfold as many as were killed on 9/11 and in a country that had nothing to do with 9/11. Oops. Meanwhile in Afghanistan we're building roads and schools we can't afford to build in our own country. Oh boy!

The world is hungry for some good news because the bad news feels so overwhelming.

Once upon a time Jesus got some bad news. King Herod, the Roman Empire's puppet ruler, had just beheaded John the Baptizer, Jesus' cousin and fellow insurgent for the kingdom of heaven. And if Herod was out to cut the head off a growing insurgency, Jesus and his companions could be next. The Jesus movement was nonviolent. Rome's wasn't. The empire wanted world peace. It would kill anyone who got in its way.

When the news is bad, what are you going to do?

> *Now when Jesus heard this, he withdrew from there in a boat to a deserted place by himself. But when the crowds heard it, they followed him on foot. When he went ashore, he saw a great crowd; and he had compassion for them and cured their sick.*
>
> *When it was evening, the disciples came and said, "This is a deserted place, and the hour is now late; send the crowds away so that they may go into the villages and buy food for themselves." Jesus said to them, "They need not go away; you*

give them something to eat." They replied, "We have nothing here but five loaves and two fish." He said, "Bring them here to me.

Taking the five loaves and the two fish, he looked up to heaven, and blessed and broke the loaves, and gave them to the disciples, and the disciples gave them to the crowds. And all ate and were filled; and they took up what was left over of the broken pieces, twelve baskets full. And those who ate were about five thousand men, besides women and children.

When the news is bad, what are you going to do?

Jesus took the little he had, blessed it, broke it open, and gave it away. He fed 5,000 people. *Take, bless, break, and give*. That's the heart of Christian practice. The way to world peace is the way of love. It's a slow way. It's a long way. It's hard, but grace abounds.

I read the news today, oh boy, and then remembered George who lives up the street and lost two sons within a month. I stopped by to see how he was doing. He'd been wrestling with a grieving spirit.

How do you mend a broken heart? I'm not sure, but I'm pretty sure you take the little you have in your hands, bless it, break it open, and give it away. Maybe it's a word of comfort. More likely it's a listening heart. But whatever it is, it becomes a blessing.

Blessings are gifts but some don't come easily. Sometimes you have to wrestle to get one. You wrestle with what's troublesome in your world, like Jacob grappling for his life through the night with some tenacious, dark power within him (Genesis 32:22–31). You wrestle with longings that ache in your heart. You struggle with questions and more questions and refuse to let go until you find a blessing. The struggle may wound you. It may cause you to limp. Still you walk forward, but more humbly than before. You walk on. You walk humbly as a wounded healer ready to bless and be blessed.

You read the news today, oh boy, and then remembered a friend scheduled for surgery on Tuesday. You read the news today, oh boy, and then remembered a neighbor who lost her job. You remembered a child whose dog had died. You remembered a widow trudging under a cloud. You remembered your brother (or was it your sister?) long neglected. You remembered a student looking for a job. You remembered an immigrant struggling to survive in a new land. You remembered a prisoner without a friend in the world.

You read the news of the world today, oh boy, and then remembered the world at hand. You remembered the world in which you move and live and have your being. The world you brush past everyday.

How do you feed a hungry world, a world hungry for love? I'm not sure, but I'm pretty sure you take the little you have in your hands, bless it, break it open, and give it away. Maybe it's a piece of bread. Maybe it's a word of comfort. More likely it's a listening heart. As it turns out, the world is hungry; hungry for someone who will simply listen and heed the longing of their hearts. ❧

WINTER 2011

SILENT PAWS

Do not fear; do not let your hands grow weak. I will deal with all your oppressors. I will save the lame and gather the outcast and will change their shame into praise. I will bring you home.
—The Prophet Zephaniah

It's been a grim couple of years in more ways than one for many of us here and elsewhere. Here's a story that might make your way a little less grim and perhaps a little more expectant. The subject of this story, a Vietnam vet, gave me permission to tell it.

He had been in and out of VA medical and psychiatric units for more than 25 years in several different states. He tried and failed to take his own life. He'd been in prison. He'd been declared permanently and totally disabled, even though he looked healthy and fit. He was surviving on about $10,000 a year. He had no family to speak of. He had a few friends and one mysterious cat.

He came to me in order to get a second opinion on that cat. A friend had referred him to me. He told me his friend said that I could be trusted. But he wanted some proof. He wanted to know if I was a doctor. Yes, I told him. I have a doctorate of ministry from Princeton Seminary, but I can't fix bodies or prescribe medication.

That's OK, he said. He just wanted to be sure I was educated because, as it turned out, he was well educated in philosophy, psychology, sociology, literature, and religion, and he was about to entrust me with his complicated physical and mental history.

I don't know exactly what happened to him in Vietnam, but I know enough Vietnam vets to know that post-traumatic stress disorder (PTSD) is an accurate if vague diagnosis. Many vets return from war with severe mental and emotional impairment. It's one of the enormous costs of war.

Which is why presidents must be honest with themselves and the nation when it comes to war. Is it truly a just war, Mr. President, or just a war to feed the voracious appetite of what President Eisenhower called the military-industrial complex? Is it a just war, Mr. President, or just another war to preserve the plush American way of life at any cost? War is not a video game. The president and Congress must renounce duplicity and speak honestly with the American people. The costs of war are enormous. The evidence of that was looking me in the eye.

I don't know exactly what happened to this veteran in the VA system, but I know enough vets, including my own nephew, to know that, as good as VA centers are, getting the help you need can take years of humiliating battles.

The man in my office bore deep wounds. He slumped under a heavy load. But clearly he was a fighter, a survivor.

Over the course of 40 years he had investigated various religious, spiritual, and ethical traditions hoping to find a mission or purpose for his life, the kind of focused mission and clear purpose he had as a soldier. He searched and searched but came up empty.

To make a long story short, let me just say: A year or so ago he decided to eliminate hope from his life. He saw no point in it. He reminded me that "hope" was the last thing released from Pandora's box of woes and misery. Hope came out last. So, is hope the ultimate salvation or the ultimate curse of humankind? He had come to see, as many others have come to see, that hope can be a cruel hoax, a sick joke.

This man lived without hope for a year, going through the motions, just staying alive until that wore thin. He resigned himself to die. He embraced death.

And then something happened.

As he lay on his bed that night, awaiting his death, counting his final minutes, he suddenly woke up. His cat was tapping his cheek with its paw—something that cat had never done before. Then he heard a whisper. He would later come to believe that whisper was the spirit of courage, or as he said, the Holy Spirit. The whisper said: *Not what, how.*

That was it. *Not what, how.*

I asked him what those words meant to him. It meant, he said, it's not what I do that matters; it's how I live. There is no mission or purpose per se; it's all about living life fully in this moment. Not what, how.

He thought that cat and that whisper had been a "religious experience," and he said so to his VA psychiatrist soon after. The psychiatrist, he said, told him it was a hallucination prompted by a neurological disorder. Now, as I said, this vet is well educated. So he couldn't completely dismiss a scientific, materialistic explanation of his experience.

And thus he came to the point of his visit: He wanted a second opinion from me. Was that cat and that whisper a religious experience, something "supernatural"?

Well, what would you have told him?

Before I answered his question, I had to ask him a question—which is what wise rabbis and ministers do: We answer a question with another question. What difference, I asked him, had that experience made in his life? That's easy, he said. It saved my life.

And that made it easier for me. After all, the ancient traditions tell of a spirit that brings life out of death, light out darkness, hope out of despair time and time again. In the hour of darkness Mother Mary whispers: Let it be. Or as the prophet Zephaniah put it:

Do not fear; do not let your hands grow weak. I will deal with all your oppressors. I will save the lame and gather the outcast and will change their shame into praise. I will bring you home, says the LORD.

Yes, this ancient but living tradition tells of a spirit that regenerates life out of death, light out darkness, hope out of despair. Sometimes we call that spirit God, sometimes Lord, sometimes Emmanuel, sometimes Tao, sometimes Wisdom, sometimes Word, sometimes Day-Spring, sometimes Great Spirit, sometimes Jesus.

Sometimes it comes to a whole nation in a time of darkness. Sometimes it comes to one soul in his or her hour of darkness.

I will bring you home.

I'm not sure how it comes, but it comes. Sometimes you see it when morning dawns. Sometimes you hear it in the midnight hour. Sometimes it comes through a voice or a piece of broken bread. And sometimes it comes on the silent paws of a cat. ❧

MIGHTY BE OUR POWERS

I have baptized you with water; but the One who is coming will baptize you with the Holy Spirit.
— The Gospel according to Mark

Recently I met a woman who is a reservist with the international Christian Peacemaking Team. Since 2005 she has spent two months every year working with victims of violence in Iraq, sometimes simply getting in the way of potential violence, unarmed.

That got me to thinking more deeply about the theory and practice of nonviolence. And that took me back 20 years to a place where AK-47 machine guns and machetes ruled the day and ruled the night. In that land, terrified people fled from armed men and boys shooting, stabbing, and hacking bodies into pieces. In that country the powers of hell had arisen on earth.

It was a time and place that I had once fleetingly heard about. But this time I looked closely at it and lingered. This time I saw the bodies strewn along roads and ditches. This time I sat with displaced families huddled in refugee camps with little to eat or drink. And this time I met a woman who in the darkest night heard a voice, saying: *Prepare the way of the Lord. Prepare the way for peace.*

Once upon a time as a child this woman had been baptized in water. Little did she know that a baptism more powerful would later overwhelm her. And little did she know that one day she would be awarded the Nobel Peace Prize.

During the dark days of this past Advent season, I immersed myself in the tragic story of the Liberian people. Few of us heard or paid much attention to the two bloody civil wars that raged there for 15 years. At that time the Persian Gulf wars grabbed our attention.

Yet the Liberian civil war is a familiar story. Civil wars rage on every continent—tribes warring against each other for control of land, resources, and governing power, not to mention inflicting revenge for old offenses and insults. It's an old story but with a modern twist. African tribes came to possess high-powered guns supplied by so-called advanced societies.

And so it was that in the early 1990s war arose in Liberia, a country to which freed slaves from America had come in the 19th century. Those freed slaves enslaved and oppressed the indigenous peoples of Liberia. Over time resentments built up and eventually fueled an uprising of indigenous tribes against the so-called Congo People, or the elite ruling tribe. Once it started, no tribe was safe from attack by another. Chaos and devastation reigned.

At the end of the first civil war, Charles Taylor became president. But peace did not come. Taylor traded blood diamonds for weapons and supplied insurgents in neighboring Sierra Leone. Meanwhile, he robbed and brutalized his own people. Another civil war broke out, and once again tens of thousands were shot, raped, and hacked to death. Chaos and devastation reigned. Again. It was as though the devil himself ruled the land.

Here we go again, cried the women of Liberia. Their fathers, husbands, sons, and brothers were off once again to kill, mutilate, and rape—over and over and over again.

It was in that dark and gloomy time that a certain young woman named Leymah Gbowee heard a voice: *Get the women of the church together to pray.*

Who me? You've made a mistake, Gbowee muttered.

Even though she was a baptized child of the church, Leymah had gone badly astray, or so she thought. She felt unworthy to be an instrument of the Holy One. Nevertheless, she obeyed the voice.

And so, Gbowee assembled and addressed the women of the church. They were sick and tired of war and feeling useless and disempowered. After all, men had all the guns. And men held all the power in their land, or so the women thought. They were about to discover a power more mighty, a force greater than the devil's guns.

Among the Christian women that day was a Muslim woman. She came to the podium and there on the spot pledged to rally the Muslim women of Liberia to join the Christian women in praying for and standing up for peace.

And that's what happened.

It was unprecedented.

Gbowee's story is told in the book *Mighty Be Our Powers: How Sisterhood, Prayer, and Sex Changed a Nation at War* and in an award-winning documentary film *Pray the Devil Back to Hell.*

As it turns out, Gbowee and other women leaders had been inspired by Gandhi, Martin Luther King Jr., and Mennonite theologian John Howard Yoder. But they were also inspired by Esther, the woman of Jewish lore who fasted and prayed to save her own people from a state-sponsored massacre.

At first a dozen women, then hundreds, and then thousands forsook their submissive cultural roles, set aside their favored colorful garments, and put on plain white T-shirts emblazoned with the Women in Peacebuilding Network logo. They stood together. They stood tall in the public squares of Monrovia, the capital of Liberia.

The women organized. They trained. They strategized. They kept at it in good times and bad times. They kept at it for years until the warlords and President Taylor were shamed into signing a peace treaty in 2003, which led to the presence of UN peacekeepers, which led to democratic elections in 2005, which led to the first woman president of an African nation, Ellen Johnson Sirleaf. In her inauguration address, Sirleaf praised the brave work of Liberian Women for Peace.

Mighty be our powers. We will pray the devil back to hell.

Nonviolent resistance to evil is not easy. It's certainly not easier than violent resistance. It's harder.

When you think about it, armed violence is pretty childish. *Bang, bang. Boom, boom. You're dead.* Violence breeds more violence. Its seeds multiply. Nonviolence breeds nonviolence. Its seeds multiply too.

Nonviolent resistance to evil is hard work. It requires grownups with strong hearts, minds, and bodies. Yes, it's harder to wage peace than it is to wage war. But it's worth it. Which is one reason the world still remembers and reveres Jesus 2,000 years later. He was killed while waging peace.

Yes, many armed warriors are brave and should be honored for their bravery and sacrifices. But unarmed warriors for peace are also brave, if not more so. Read Gbowee's story and you'll see what I mean. ❧

SUMMER 2012

RESURRECTION AS EVOLUTION

Jesus on the Eastern Shore

They were startled and terrified, and thought that they were seeing a ghost. They gave him a piece of broiled fish. Jesus took it and ate in their presence.
— LUKE 24

If you believe in the grand and glorious story of evolution, it's hard to quibble with the Resurrection. I mean, really. If you're OK with the mind-boggling, jaw-dropping 4.5-billion-year-old story of nature unfolding on this once lifeless planet, well, what's not to believe in yet another amazing knock-your-socks-off surprise called "the Resurrection"? Unfortunately, Christendom turned it into a freak show. It's actually as "natural" as can be.

But before we look at the Resurrection with fresh eyes, let's look again at the grand and glorious story of evolution.

This planet could have been called Water. For eons nothing but water covered this big rock we call Earth. And then 4 billion or so years ago something happened.

In the soupy water something stirred. Out of molecules a simple cell with an urge to merge and replicate arose—not out of thin air but close to it.

It wasn't much. But it was a start.

Had there been choirs at the time, an anthem would have resounded: *The simple cell has triumphed! Hallelujah!*

And, surprise, surprise, simple cells could do things mere molecules couldn't.

One thing led to another, including nucleated cells. Eventually bushy vegetation emerged in rivers, streams, and oceans. An anthem could have resounded: *Vegetation has triumphed! Hallelujah!*

And, surprise, surprise, plants could do things mere cells couldn't.

Under the sea one thing led to another, including creatures with fins and tails. And then one day a curious creature slithered onto land and said: *WOW. Look at that lush garden of delight! Yummy, yummy.*

By the way, all creatures had just two things on their minds. One was eating. And I'm pretty sure you can guess the other.

Anyway, that slithering creature procreated. Some of its descendants developed legs, some wings. Things were really taking off now. An anthem could have resounded: *Animals have triumphed! Hallelujah!*

And, surprise, surprise, animals could do things mere plants couldn't.

As each new emergent kingdom or realm arose on the earth, it brought characteristics of the realm below and then introduced an amazing surprise, something unforeseen and unpredictable until it was revealed.

And thus from the realm of animals emerged human beings, animal-like creatures with, surprise, surprise, a near infinite capacity to create and destroy but also a capacity to love. Evolution of *consciousness*—and with it *cultural* evolution—would now outpace *biological* evolution on this planet.

An anthem could have resounded: *Humans have triumphed!* But it would be quickly followed by a dirge: *Oh, my God, look what we've done to the earth and each other.*

In a mucked up lovely river,
I cast my little fly.
I look at that river and smell it
And it makes me want to cry.
Oh to clean our dirty planet,
Now there's a noble wish,
And I'm puttin' my shoulder to the wheel
'Cause I wanna catch some fish.
(Greg Brown, "Spring Wind")

And that brings me to the story of the Resurrection of Jesus on the Eastern Shore.

Jesus was killed, in part, for revealing another realm in the making, called in his day "the kingdom [or kin-dom] of God," a realm of being that would replicate and flourish, but not by sexual procreation, as did other realms. This new communally integrated life form would flourish—and here comes another amazing surprise out of the story of evolution—by *conscious, intentional collaborations with Love.*

God is love and those who abide in love abide in God.

As you know, love isn't just a feeling. It's action. And justice, as it turns out, is the social or political expression of love. Love and justice belong together.

This higher consciousness and capacity manifested in the Resurrection story is a relatively recent leap forward in terms of the evolutionary timeline. For the first time humans *witnessed* evolutionary emergence not in fossil records but with their own eyes. Not surprisingly they were left pretty much speechless, tripping over words, stretching language to the breaking point.

They thought they were seeing a ghost.

Whatever arose in that Resurrection arose into human consciousness as real as can be and started transforming ordinary people into bold lovers. The gospel story of the Resurrection itself is a parable of new possibilities within the material and biological world.

Out of the human realm something new is emerging, a life form with a capacity for forgiveness instead of retaliation; nonviolence instead of violence; reconciliation instead of enmity; and an amazing capacity to include more and more people, more and more racial, ethnic, sexual, and religious diversity within a community. The Resurrection spirit lures us to become less tribal and more global.

This emerging form of communal life is known by many names. My own tradition calls it "the Christ" or "Cosmic Christ." But by whatever name, you can be sure it doesn't arise without bold love and deep suffering on behalf of others. It brings with it wounded hearts, scarred hands and feet. It arises not from the death of the human organism itself but from the death of the "old self" or ego. That kind of death leads to new birth and integration into this new life form. Just as a two-dimensional square is not diminished when integrated into a three-dimensional cube, so the person who surrenders to Love is not diminished but glorified.

Anything that stands in the way of this widening circle of love is (quite simply) *sin*. Racism, sexism, homophobia, and greed may linger for years to come, but we've seen their defeat in the Christ who has triumphed over sin and death.

In case you hadn't heard, the Resurrected Christ made an appearance earlier this year on the Eastern Shore. It happened this way.

In response to the fish kills in the Shenandoah River, The Downstream Project produced a documentary on the history and environmental problems of the Shenandoah and the

Chesapeake Bay, including industrial pollution, sediment and nutrient pollution from the loss of riparian areas from livestock grazing, poultry processing, and human waste, which threaten an entire ecosystem. A grim forecast indeed.

This past March, Bill Howard, executive director of The Downstream Project, and his coworkers accompanied the Chesapeake Bay Foundation and a group of cattle and dairy farmers from the Shenandoah Valley to Tangier Island, in the middle of the bay. The farmers spent three days getting to know some fishermen. Hostility had been brewing between the two groups for years.

Howard put it this way: "The valley farmers set crab pots and tonged oysters, shared seafood, and stories of their remarkably similar and challenging lives. The farmers became more aware of how their agricultural practices affect the quality of the bay and the livelihoods of the watermen. With efforts like this and organizations like the Chesapeake Bay Foundation, I hold out great hope."

And there you have it: another incarnation of the Resurrection Spirit. It's not about ghosts. It's about real things, real water, real fish, and real people transformed by amazing love, forgiveness, and reconciliation. It's about putting your shoulder to the wheel because you wanna catch some fish—for yourself and for a hungry world. ❧

SONG OF PEACE FOR 9/11

Make me a channel of your peace.
— St. Francis of Assisi

Question: Do you know the name of the person who gave the winter coat off his back to a homeless woman and then said: *She needed it more than me.* If you're thinking St. Francis, you're close.

Hint: This person cared for recovering alcoholics, the homeless, the hungry, the sick, injured, and grieving. He cared for immigrants, gays, and lesbians. He once knelt beside a man dying of AIDS and when that dying man asked if God hated him, the one kneeling picked him up, kissed him, and silently rocked him in his arms. If you're still thinking St. Francis, you're still close because St. Francis was known to have embraced lepers as though they were the Beloved Christ.

Alright. One more hint: This person is the same person who on 9/11 rushed into the North Tower of the World Trade Center to offer prayers for the dying only to die himself from flying debris. That person would become the first officially recorded fatality of 9/11. No, of course, it's not St. Francis. It is Father Mychal Judge, a priest in the Order of Franciscan Minors and longtime chaplain of the New York City Fire Department.

Father Judge wasn't born with an instinct to rush into burning buildings. But, as it turns out, he was nurtured in the spirit of St. Francis, a spirit encapsulated in the prayer attributed to the saint. And, by the way, you don't have to be a priest or even a Christian to make it your prayer or, better yet, to make it your true vocation.

Make me a channel of your peace:
Where there is hatred, let me bring your love,
Where there is injury, your pardon, Lord,
And where there's doubt true faith in you.
Make me a channel of your peace:
Where there's despair in life, let me bring hope,
Where there is darkness, only light,
And where there's sadness, ever joy.

Father Judge wasn't the first or the last to give up his coat that another might be warm or give a meal that another might eat. He wasn't the first or the last to bring light into darkness, hope into despair, or pardon to the injured. He wasn't the first to be a channel of peace or to urge others to love the whole world and not just their own kind or their own people or their own nation.

There were many before and will be many after, in part, because parents, schools, and faith communities intentionally and consistently cultivate compassion against all odds. That's no guarantee we'll all turn out like Father Judge, but it's a step in the right direction.

It takes more, much more, than formal classes, lectures, or sermons to cultivate compassion. It takes practice in all the moments of a day.

What better antidote to the lingering trauma of 9/11 than this affirmation: *The way of love has not been forsaken. The way of light and hope has not been forgotten. The way of forgiveness is still being taught in a post-9/11 world.*

No, forgiveness is not easy. And no, it doesn't mean you forget what happened to you. And no, it doesn't mean you let people walk over you or beat you up. To forgive, or to be willing to forgive, means you believe the past can be transformed by grace. It means we can be set free from crippling resentments.

Eleven years ago on September 11, enemies of our nation danced for joy as we reeled from a devastating attack. They weren't the first or last to dance upon the grave of an enemy.

In May last year, nearly 11 years after 9/11, Americans danced for joy over the death of Osama bin Laden. Sweet revenge. But, of course, it wasn't sweet enough to cure the aching in many hearts.

Glee over the death of one's enemy is as old as the hills. Here's a song 3,000 years old: *I will sing to the Lord, for he has triumphed gloriously; horse and rider he has thrown into the sea. The Lord is a warrior.*

For those who might think otherwise: That is not from the Quran. It's from the Bible.

Does God intervene that way—to kill some and spare others, or is that what *certain people* in a *childish* frame of mind *think* God is like? Some of our ancestors thought so, as do some of our current national leaders. But it doesn't mean we have to think like them. It's childish. It's OK to be *childlike* in faith; but *childishness* does not befit an adult.

Of course, childishness in our species should be no surprise; we are quite recent arrivals on this planet and have yet to learn our manners not to mention unlearn tribalistic ways. To think violence will end violence is childish. I don't care how sophisticated our rationalizations—*Hate cannot drive out hate. Only love can do that.*

Eleven years ago, two weeks after 9/11, my wife, Paula, and I began a journey around the world. It was a sabbatical planned nearly a year before. We visited 10 different countries over 100 days. Few Americans were traveling at that time. Most tours had been canceled. Many tourists stayed home.

In each country we visited—from New Zealand to Kenya to Greece, Spain, and Ireland—our hosts and strangers greeted us with words of deep sympathy for America. We were honored and humbled to receive such gestures of goodwill on behalf of our country.

It seemed the world was on the threshold of a new day. America's gaping wound had opened up a moment of grace. The world saw the mightiest nation hurting and humbled; no longer invincible but, just like every other nation, vulnerable to profound suffering.

In that poignant moment a song buried deep in the world's collective heart arose. Not a song of victory or vindication or war; but rather a song of peace, a song of peace for all the nations. And if you heard it, please don't forget it. Never let it go. It's sung in many different ways. Here's one.

This Is My Song

This is my song, O God of all the nations,
A song of peace for lands afar and mine.
This is my home, the country where my heart is;
Here are my hopes, my dreams, my holy shrine;
But other hearts in other lands are beating
With hopes and dreams as true and high as mine.

My country's skies are bluer than the ocean
And sunlight beams on cloverleaf and pine;
But other lands have sunlight, too, and clover,
And skies are everywhere as blue as mine.
O hear my song, O God of all the nations,
A song of peace for their land and for mine.

May truth and freedom come to every nation;
may peace abound where strife has raged so long;
that each may seek to love and build together,
a world united, righting every wrong;
a world united in its love for freedom,
proclaiming peace together in one song.

Lloyd Stone, 1934 ❧

THE END OF THE WORLD

(Read before December 21)

In talking about the fate of the earth, we know that its fate is really up for grabs. There are no guarantees as to its future. It is a question of our own critical choices.
—Miriam Therese MacGillis

In case you hadn't heard, there's no need to worry about the fiscal cliff looming at the end of this year. Forget the cliff. And forget the end of the year. We're not going to get to the end of the year. The world ends 10 days before that.

According to the venerable Mayans, the world ends December 21, which means, in part, you don't have to worry about last-minute Christmas shopping this year. So there's a silver lining for you.

Still, the end of the world could be a real bummer. But there are worse things. For instance, the maker of Twinkies is going out of business. Of course, for some the end of Twinkies might as well be the end of the world. Talk about cosmic convergences. I don't think even the Mayans saw that coming. For some things you really do need Google.

The "end of the world," as it turns out, may not be THE END as in UTTER AND COMPLETE ANNIHILATION. In fact, one interpretation of the Mayan calendar is that the world will start *recycling* on December 21 rather than *ending once and for all*. Which could actually be worse. That would mean we'd have to live through all the stuff we've already lived through once—like the bubonic plague, leisure suits, Bill Clinton, and the Bee Gees.

But then, there is the possibility that the venerable Mayans could be wrong. I mean how many of these predictions have been right? Ever?!

Before the Civil War there was William Miller and the Millerites, who sold all their earthly possessions in 1843 and gathered on a mountaintop. They camped out waiting for Jesus, who would snatch them up (rapture) just before he destroyed the world. But alas, Miller Time was not Happy Hour for the Millerites. They ran out of food and patience and trudged down the mountain to restart their lives with nothing left but shame.

Remember Y2K? As I recall that turned out to be a pretty cool, rolling-time-zone party.

Remember Hal Lindsey's *The Late Great Planet Earth* scare in the 1970s? He's still living off the sales of that book.

Remember David Koresh and the Davidians in *Wacko*, Texas?

Remember Harold Camping?

Radio evangelist Camping spent a lifetime studying the Bible's secret codes and thus was able to predict that the world would be destroyed on May 21, 2011. Many people were convinced and sold their possessions to wait the massive airlift (rapture!) just before the destruction of the world. It never happened.

By the way, Jesus was once asked to predict the end of the world and he replied: *No one knows!* As in NO ONE. I'm not saying Jesus is *God*, but a lot of *these characters* do think Jesus is God, which makes you wonder how they got to *know more than God.* (I'm just sayin'!)

Anyway, back to Harold Camping. Camping broadcast his prediction to millions, risked his reputation, and was understandably depressed on May 22 when he woke up in his own bed. I don't know if it's true, but I heard that his neighbor paid Camping a visit the day after, put a consoling arm around him, and said: *Harold, don't worry. It's not the end of the world.*

But the thing is: *The world did end*. For Mr. Camping. His world of certainty and delusions ended.

Soon after, he humbly and publicly admitted his arrogance and ignorance. Which he called a "sin." I give him credit for that. People make mistakes. Some are harmless like his, but others aren't so harmless, like the prediction made 10 years ago by a certain Dick Cheney: "Oil revenues will pay for this war." Remember that one?

I don't know if that was a sin, but it sure was a crime.

And it led to the death of thousands and to the end of a certain world. Overnight the United States of America lost the respect of half the nations.

One world ended.

Another began.

The American military machine could now put its boots on the ground and fire its drones without regard for another country's sovereignty or a person's citizenship. It was a new world. We became the policemen of that world, with military bases or stations in 173 nations (out of 186).

Now, I happen to be a home-team fan. So if some nation must police the world, I'd rather it be us. But the thing is, it doesn't have to be any one nation. We don't need an empire. We don't need a military bigger than all the next 14 biggest militaries *combined*, especially since *most of those are allies*. Go figure. And when you go figure, you'll figure out a lot of good and wholesome things we could do in our nation when that kind of money and human power comes home.

Worlds end all the time. And that's not always a bad thing.

Worlds, after all, are human inventions. It may be one planet but there are many different worlds on it. Some small, some large. Some more fair and compassionate than others.

You might say a certain world of gross inequality, exclusion, and mean-spiritedness is ending in America. The recent election was a sign. Even conservative pundits can see it. As Michael Gerson put it in the *Washington Post*: "The next Republican campaign will need to be capable of complex adjustments of ideology, policy and rhetoric. And it will need one more thing: a candidate with a genuine, creative passion for *inclusion*. Perhaps our greatest need at this time is a commitment to the common good and *a particular concern for the poor and vulnerable."* (italics added)

That attitude bodes well for our nation. A different world is arising in America. For one thing, we've become a nation of minorities. The white majority is now (or soon will be) a minority, which means cooperation and compromise are more necessary than ever.

Marriage equality and sexual orientation are fast becoming nonissues in our nation. Openly gay men and women are elected routinely to national and state government.

Twenty women serve in the Senate. Buddhist, Christians, Hindus, Jews, Muslims, and "none-of-the-above" serve in Congress.

It even looks like marijuana may be decriminalized, controlled, and taxed like alcohol was after Prohibition. That itself would set a lot of benign (and mellow) prisoners free, save tax payers a ton of money, put a dent in the deficit, and allow law enforcement agencies to pursue truly dangerous criminals.

A new world is rising. Even "liberal" is no longer a four-letter word. Who could have guessed?

But let's not be fooled. The new world arising is not completely righteous or good. A pervasive and pernicious police state is afoot in our land. Militarism consumes us. Bigotry and discrimination have not been vanquished. Humans are sold. Animals are mistreated. Violence and greed thrive. All is not well.

Not yet.

There is much work to be done to bring peace and good will to all on earth. ❧

GUNS IN AMERICA

A Call to Prayer and One or Two More Things

I believe that even amid today's mortar bursts and whining bullets, there is still hope for a brighter tomorrow.
— Martin Luther King Jr.

Cain killed Abel.
— Genesis

Ever since the Sandy Hook Elementary School massacre, gun violence has been much debated. We must work and pray to end these recurring national nightmares.

But it's not just Sandy Hook.

And it's not just Aurora, Colorado, and Virginia Tech.

It's also 500 gun deaths in Chicago last year and the year before that and the year before that, many of them children—black children who, evidently, aren't worthy of national news or presidential commissions.

It's not just Sandy Hook and Chicago. *It's that Americans are 20 times as likely to be killed by a gun than is someone from another developed country.* (Max Fisher, *Washington Post,* December 14, 2012)

It's not that Americans are more homicidal and suicidal than other people. It may just be that we have far more guns—5 percent of the world's population holding 50 percent of the world's guns.

It's not just about Sandy Hook or Chicago or *30,000 gun-related deaths per year, half of them suicides*. And it's not just about our citizens stocking up on assault weapons.

It's also about a *culture of violence.*

It's Hollywood. It's video games. It's our Department of Defense stocking inordinate piles of weapons, bombs, and aircraft carriers—all in greater numbers than the next 10 nations combined!

How can the leaders of the administration stand up and say with a straight face: *We can't trust our citizens with assault weapons.* How can they say that? How can they say that when *our military has enough weapons to destroy the world several times over?*

Who else is flying drones over other nations?

Who else is killing school children from the air?

How can the rest of the world trust US *with weapons of mass destruction?*

Apparently, some of our own citizens don't trust our government either!

The day after the Sandy Hook massacre, I was standing in a grocery line when an iconic little old lady behind me said to her friend: *I'm so glad I got my gun before this happened. I'm afraid I'd never get one now*. That kind of thinking made guns fly off the shelves.

Fear. And more fear. And it's growing like cancer.

Many of our fellow citizens really and truly are afraid. And not just of burglars and muggers. Some fear our very own government and its agents.

Two years ago the FBI arrested members of a certain, self-proclaimed, heavily armed and well-regulated militia in Michigan who were prepared to murder law enforcement agents in order to provoke insurrection against the government. *And that's but one of many paramilitary groups armed to the teeth and afoot in our country*. I'm pretty sure that type of "well-regulated militia" was not what our nation's founders had in mind in the Second Amendment.

Still, the Second Amendment is to be cherished—in its entirety. It means we are *citizens*, not *subjects*.

Ironically, it seems a lot of people who think they are *brave citizens* have unwittingly become *subjects*. They've been duped. They have become slaves of fear, cynically manipulated by fear-mongering, money-grubbing tyrants, including the propaganda of a certain, once noble organization now thriving on the devil's lie that *guns don't kill*. Clever slogan. But, really, what sane person believes such a thing?!

Guns kill.

Period.

Wake up and smell the blood on the schoolhouse floor!

It's true, not every gun owner is gripped by fear. By far, most are hunting and sports enthusiasts well trained in the safe use of a handgun or rifle. Maybe one day those types will stand up to the tyrants and tell them to *shut up, back off, and sit down*. The vast majority of Americans would applaud.

In case you haven't noticed, our nation is in the grip of a demonic fetish. Sinister powers sway elected officials with the root of all evil, *the love of money*. "In Guns We Trust" is written all over that currency.

Just when you thought it was a "political issue" it turns out to be moral and spiritual. It's about trust. It's about giving your heart to something worthy of your heart. And that's where prayer comes in.

Prayer—as Martin Luther King Jr. believed—is one way to confront a demonic situation. It's not the only way, but it is a powerful way.

So, yes, we should pray our hearts out. And try everything else.

New laws banning military-style weapons and requiring universal background checks can be effective *but only up to a point.* Laws are not enough. Laws are necessary but not sufficient.

Mental health screening, including medication and reporting can be effective *but only up to a point.* Finding a potential mass murderer by psychological screening, as one psychiatrist put it, is like finding a needle in a haystack. Screening is necessary but not sufficient.

Long, long before Sandy Hook, our nation could have been providing far more mental health resources for children and youth. For the price of one aircraft carrier we could put full-time mental health counselors in every school to detect and treat dangerous aggression at an early age. Mental health care is necessary but not sufficient.

Gun violence is deeper than laws, screening, or counseling can touch. It's deep as the human heart.

According to the Great Ancestors' mythic tale, the first human child killed his baby brother. And the killing hasn't stopped.

According to the tale, out of unresolved anger over feeling rejected and unloved, Cain killed Abel. It's a folktale, not history. It portrays our existential predicament as human beings.

All of us are vulnerable to injury, anger, and revenge. How we react depends largely on circumstances. Many people are born into social, economic, political, and family conditions that *greatly* exacerbate every frustration with life. Violence is then easily unchained.

It's not fair. Yet neither is it decreed to remain unchanged.

After killing his brother, Cain wandered east of Eden and built the first city—a community—where he could feel safe from all that violence lurking out there. Cain could have posted guards at every gate and put a loaded gun in every teacher's desk, but as long as Cain was inside, the city would never be safe.

I'm all for changing the human heart. But while we're holding our breath, changing a few laws and certain circumstances could help. ❧

AMERICA THE BEAUTIFUL

Same-Sex Marriage on the Thoroughfare for Freedom

O beautiful for pilgrim feet
Whose stern impassion'd stress
A thoroughfare for freedom beat
Across the wilderness
America! America!
God mend thine ev'ry flaw,
Confirm thy soul in self-control,
Thy liberty in law.

America is beautiful. Just look at its vast seashores, magnificent rivers, spacious skies, purple mountain majesties, fruited plains, and amber waves of grain. It takes your breath away!

America is beautiful and was so long before it was called "America." Its people are beautiful, too.

But America's ways have not always been so beautiful or good. We have murdered, stolen, lied, raped, oppressed, and enslaved others, often in the name of God. And thus, on top of everything else, we have blasphemed. We have privileged a few at the expense of many. We have denied many their rights.

And thus, rightly and necessarily, our national hymn continually calls us to self-examination, humility, and repentance: *America! America! God, mend thy every flaw.*

Lately we've been mending one flaw, although "flaw" is too small a word for it. For it is a grave and wicked injustice that the Declaration of Independence was bound to expose one day.

We hold these truths to be self-evident that all men are created equal and endowed by their Creator with certain unalienable rights that among these are Life, Liberty and the pursuit of Happiness.

And that, too, is a beautiful part of America. For 237 years our Declaration of Independence has been a beacon for the world.

The founders may have meant *males only* but the spirit in the letter meant *women*, too. The founders may have meant *white people* only but the spirit meant *people of color*, too. The founders may have meant *heterosexuals* only but the spirit meant *homosexuals*, too. The founders, like all poets and prophets, said more than they knew.

As Jesus said, the Spirit of God blows where it will. And recently she has blown across this land like a cyclone knocking down barriers against equality of opportunity. But it takes more than spirit. It takes laws to confirm our liberties.

America! America! Confirm thy soul in self-control, Thy liberty in law.

In more and more states, gays and lesbians now enjoy the same protection and benefits granted to heterosexual couples. Many societies and nations have not allowed such freedom and equality to blossom, and although it's true we are behind many others, we are at last, however slowly, beating a thoroughfare for freedom across the wilderness. It's reached Connecticut, Delaware, Iowa, Maine, Maryland, Massachusetts, Minnesota, New Hampshire, New York, Rhode Island, Vermont, and Washington—as well as the District of Columbia and three Native American tribes.

Liberty is being *confirmed in law*. For heaven's sake, set off some fireworks! Let the heavens rejoice and the earth be glad.

On Independence Day celebrate liberty and love in all its many expressions.

Look around. God loves diversity, revels in abundance and extravagance. I mean, look at *the whole shebang*, which is to say, the universe and this planet we call Earth. Whatever else you might say about the Great Spirit, you can say this: *She loves diversity.*

Helium wasn't enough. She had to make hydrogen, oxygen, nitrogen, and a whole lot more. One star wasn't enough. He had to make billions and billions more and many galaxies besides. Stingrays weren't enough. It had to have a billion other fish. Eagles weren't enough. Spinach wasn't enough (thank God!). Daffodils weren't enough. Apples weren't enough. Giraffes weren't enough. One kind of human wasn't enough. And one kind of sexuality wasn't enough.

Prodigious love has been filling the universe ever since hydrogen felt the urge to merge with oxygen. A wild and wonderful world is in the making and, wonder of wonders, we have eyes to see, ears to hear, hearts to sing, and hands to reach out and touch it with love and respect.

The Creator loves diversity. And in case you hadn't noticed, the only thing the Beloved loves more than diversity is community—people and things living together in harmony. It's really not enough to merely tolerate diversity. Go out and embrace it for all it's worth.

As a Christian minister and a brother in this wild and wonderful human family, I say this to my gay, lesbian, bisexual, transgender, and questioning brothers and sisters: Far too many churches have scorned, judged, demeaned, bullied, and condemned you—in the precious name of the beloved Christ—just for being who you are. They have recited lies. They have incited fear instead of cultivating tolerance, understanding, acceptance, and love.

But all who speak in the name of Christ are not necessarily of Christ or of the way of Jesus. Jesus said: *I am the way, the truth, and the life.* By that, I believe, he meant "love" is *the way to live.* Regrettably, many Christians have taken his beautiful and welcoming words and turned them into bricks and swords.

Jesus is the heart of the Christian tradition, and Jesus said next to nothing about sex or sexuality. But Jesus did say a lot about love. *Love one another as I have loved you.*

Jesus did not come to condemn but to save, to save us from fear and hatred. The *way of Jesus* is not a way out of this world into another. It is a way of being in this world. It's a way of being in love—feeding the hungry, healing the sick, mending the brokenhearted, and befriending the outcast.

Every intimate, committed relationship between one adult and another deserves the opportunity for the blessing, protection, and benefits of a solemn covenant, a covenant that encourages fidelity to the sacred promises of love. *And that means marriage.*

Regrettably most churches, including my own, have yet to catch up to the states, let alone the Spirit. May God help us mend our every flaw and purge our sins against others.

We all mess up. America has messed up big time. But where there is grace, honesty, and humility, there is hope.

This July Fourth we have reason to be proud and grateful to live in America. No, things aren't nearly well or safe enough for LGBTQ citizens; in fact, far from it in our own state. This year, however, as we celebrate our nation's Declaration of Independence we can also celebrate with our gay and lesbian brothers and sisters this new possibility, the dawning of their own new day of freedom and equality. At last. ❧

JIM CROW IS BACK

Mass Incarceration in Colorblind America

Wash yourselves; make yourselves clean; remove the evil of your doings from before my eyes; cease to do evil, learn to do good; seek justice, rescue the oppressed, defend the orphan, plead for the widow.
— The Prophet Isaiah

My son is serving time in a federal prison. I visit him often. He's white, and that makes him a minority in the United State prison system, where more than half of the 2.2 million inmates are black or brown. The guards, on the other hand, are nearly all white.

What's wrong with this picture?

Unless you believe that people of color are genetically predisposed to crime, you have to suspect that the social and economic conditions into which many are born provoke criminal behavior or that law enforcement is not colorblind—or both.

You'd have to be blind not to see that when it comes to the criminal justice system, *race matters.* I've seen the extreme racial disparity in federal and state prisons. And that, in part, led me to Michelle Alexander's book, *The New Jim Crow: Mass Incarceration in an Age of Colorblindness.*

Of course, in one sense, "race" is an artificial construct invented by pseudoscience in the 19th century. We are all one family, one species with various and irrelevant shades of brown skin. But, unfortunately, we've come to make a big, big deal of pigmentation and to base unrighteous policies on it.

If only race didn't matter. But it does—at least here in America.

The idea that we may never reach a state of perfect racial equality is not cause for alarm, says Alexander. *What is troubling, however, is the real possibility that we, as a society, will choose not to care.*

I am writing this because I'd like you to care, care enough to get informed about this national tragedy, about this new kind of racial oppression in the United States—what Alexander calls the "New Jim Crow." It's based on the mass incarceration of African American men fueled by a trillion-dollar "war on drugs."

Since that "war" amped up in the 1980s, the number of inmates rose from several hundred thousand to more than 2 million, nearly a 2,000 percent increase in the incarceration rate. We are 5 percent of the world population with 25 percent of the world's prisoners. And we're building even more and bigger prisons, as if we had no common sense or imagination.

Nearly half of all young black men are either in prison or under probation. More African American men are in the American corrections system now than were enslaved in 1850.

Being in prison is bad enough. But the stigma that follows an ex-con for a lifetime can be even worse, says Alexander. The lifelong penalties for even a nonviolent drug conviction have created a permanent second-class status for millions of Americans who are prohibited from voting, getting licensed for work, or accessing public assistance.

There's more than one way to be shackled!

Ex-inmates live on pins and needles, or we might say, under a dangling sword. Once you're marked you are never free again. The slightest and even *completely irrelevant* violation of parole or probation can cost another five to 10 years in prison with little or no recourse. Lose your job or fail to get one and you are at risk of re-incarceration. It's hard enough for white ex-cons to find work. Guess how hard it is to get a job in the inner city these days.

The system dooms to failure many ex-cons of color. And that is what Alexander identifies as a racial caste system, a system that began 500 years ago with slavery, and after the Civil War became the Jim Crow laws of explicit segregation—you know, equal but separate, including drinking fountains, bathrooms, schools, even seats on buses and trains.

The 20th-century civil rights movement prompted significant civil rights legislation including the Voting Rights Act. Those laws eliminated discriminatory practices but not irreversibly. We've seen progress but regression as well.

Still, there are reasons to be hopeful.

More and more people, including the attorney general of the United States, are waking up to this travesty of justice within the borders of our beloved country. Even those who once favored "locking 'em up and throwing away the key" are changing their minds.

It's a moral awakening but also an economic awakening. According to Nicholas Kristof of the *New York Times*, it costs the state of California more than $150,000 a year to keep a juvenile in detention. By contrast, the state spends $10,000 a year on students in school. And that's generally the case in most states.

Marc Levin, senior policy adviser for the conservative organization Right on Crime, describes the change of opinion on parole violators like this: "It used to be 'trail 'em, nail 'em, and jail 'em.' But conservatives are changing. We are now more likely to say, 'Yes, surveillance is necessary, but we also want them to succeed.' "

The wicked genius of this new caste system is that it doesn't depend on overt discrimination or racial animosity. All it requires is racial indifference to the plight of a racial minority and the illusion that the law is applied neutrally. Colorblindness can be simple blindness.

Perhaps you have heard about the disparities of sentencing and punishment for the possession of *crack* cocaine versus *powder* cocaine. It's the same drug in two slightly different forms, and yet the form used mostly by blacks reaps a much, much harsher sentence. Prison demographics tell that story.

If the war on drugs were colorblind, you'd expect drug enforcement agents to cast their dragnets over white suburbs, white professional office suites, and elite colleges *where marijuana use is known to be higher than in black ghettos*. Can you imagine what would happen if police did random "stop and frisk" on prep school or college campuses instead of the streets of inner cities? What if 50 percent of white young men were suddenly under arrest or imprisoned?

But that doesn't happen. White youth are largely given a pass on marijuana possession. Black arrests are 3 to 1 over whites; convictions are much higher.

So what if anything can we do to mitigate or eliminate this diabolical system?

The first thing is to open our eyes to the truth of its unjustness and cruelty. Change begins with knowledge. Reading Alexander's book or one of the many frequent articles in newspapers is a good place to start.

Awareness. Contrition. Repentance. Action.

The solutions aren't simple or obvious. Prisons are needed up to a point for public safety. But there is such a thing as "cruel and unusual punishment," including long mandatory sentences out of touch with reality and common sense.

According to Alexander, it will take a multiracial and multiclass mobilization to change things. But, she says, if all we do is reduce arrests and incarceration rates or modify sentencing formulas, we will not have done enough.

We need a change of heart, a transformation of our nation's soul. What the Bible calls repentance.

The change must go deep. It must reach our hearts. And like most wholesome transformations it begins with compassion. ❧

WINTER 2013

JESUS BUGS ME

Then Jesus asked, "Which of these three, do you think, was a neighbor to the man who fell into the hands of the robbers?" The lawyer replied, "The one who showed him mercy." Then Jesus said, "Go and do likewise."
— THE GOSPEL ACCORDING TO LUKE

Have you seen that bedraggled man outside of town with the sign: "HELP ME"? I don't know about you, but that guy bugs me!

That guy bugs me, and Jesus bugs me, too. *Jesus bugs me, this I know...* (Could be a new song there!)

Jesus bugs me, this I know, for the Bible tells me a story he told about a priest and Levite who saw a helpless man along the road, and they—to their everlasting shame—passed by on the other side.

When I see that bedraggled man, I just keep rolling by, cursing Jesus under my breath for his annoying "Good Samaritan" parable. If you're not careful, you'll see bedraggled people everywhere!

Forty some years ago, when I was a college student, a group of us were strolling through Chicago's Union Station licking big ice cream cones. Suddenly, Mark tossed his cone into a trashcan. The rest of us stopped in our tracks. We turned to Mark and asked, *What was wrong with that cone?*

"Nothing. Nothing, really, he said. It's just that… well, it's just that we passed a homeless man sitting on rags back there, and I couldn't keep eating ice cream knowing that guy had nothing to eat."

(Tossing away your ice cream cone will feed the hungry?! Like, really?!)

My friend Mark went on to be a Rhodes scholar, an author of a dozen books, and a distinguished professor of history at the University of Notre Dame. To this day I can't eat an ice cream cone without thinking of that homeless guy in Union Station and my friend Mark.

Mark bugs me.

I know that guy with the HELP ME sign outside of town hasn't been beaten, mugged, and robbed like the victim in the Good Samaritan story. But I know enough about the inhumanity of our social and economic systems to know that guy may, *just may*, be a victim like all those hungry children in Green County, Tennessee, described in *The Washington Post* this past summer. Who will feed those children and millions like them now that Big Ag-Business got its government subsidy and food stamp recipients got pushed aside?

You see, *knowing* about those hungry children in Tennessee and *knowing* about HIV-stricken children in Africa and *knowing* about bereaved families in Sandy Hook and war-ravaged Afghans; and *knowing* about terrified illegal immigrants and persecuted LGBT youth and profiled young African American men; and knowing about the jobless in this country and the hundred or so homeless children in Jefferson County; and *knowing* about threatened species, wetlands, rivers, farmlands, and forests; *knowing all of that and so much more*—all of it bugs me!

Sometimes I wish I didn't know so much. Sometimes I wish I'd never heard of Jesus and his goody-two-shoes Samaritan.

That Good Samaritan story bugs me, even though I'm not a "priest" or a "Levite." It bugs me because I know what Jesus means by "priest" and "Levite."

You know and I know he means people who are well-off, comfortable, powerful, and influential. He means people who *know* the right thing to do, who *could* do the right thing but don't. He means people who pass by hurting human beings because they don't want to get their hands dirty. Or because they just don't see. Or maybe they pass by because they are on their way to discuss the problem of inhumanity.

I get it. I get that I'm one of those who walk by on the other side, and I'm not happy about it. But I have some questions for Jesus that the lawyer in the story didn't ask: *What is love? What is the right thing to do and how can we be sure?*

I don't know about you, but "Who is my neighbor?" is not my question. I know that answer. I get that "neighbor" isn't about location or race or nationality. I get that. Neighbor is an attitude. Neighbor is a verb not a noun. It's being *neighborly* to any and all.

We are one family—brothers and sisters all. I get that! And because of television and the Internet, we now see bruised and wounded neighbors everywhere.

So, what's a good, sensitive, compassionate, thinking person to do?

What's the right thing to do when so many needs and needy people cry out and when victims may be faking it anyway and when help isn't always helpful and when helping just creates dependency and when helping just makes me feel good and superior for being better than slobs who don't care?

And, oh, by the way, doesn't the Bible say, "God helps those who help themselves"? Actually, no. Quite the opposite.

You see how hard this can be if you want it to be?

I don't have the answers. But I do have a few suggestions.

One: Keep calm, be still, and be *glad*. Be glad for that troubling question.

Don't let that question die.

Two: Keep calm, be still, and be *humble*. Be humble because you cannot fix the world by yourself. Rushing about doing good is more devilish than holy.

Three: Keep calm, be still, and be *grateful*. Be grateful because countless others are working to mend the world and its wounded multitudes. All kinds of people are doing good work everywhere!

Four: Keep calm, be still, and *be*. Simply be there for someone in your own small world. You can't do everything, but that doesn't mean you can't do something. And whatever you do, let it be joyful, or you won't be doing much good for yourself or anyone else. As Mother Teresa put it: "If you want to work for world peace, go home and love your family." It's true: Compassion begins at home. But it hardly ever ends there.

And finally: Keep calm, be still, and *know*. Know your own wounds. Know your own vulnerability and need of grace. We all end up "robbed and beaten" in some "roadside ditch" in one way or another, often more than once.

It's not ours always to be giving. At times it is ours to receive.

Which is to say: When you're down and out, be still and watch. The night may be long but there's a neighbor holding out a candle for you. ❧

SUMMER 2014

WE ARE ONE

Except for a Certain Goat

The National Basketball Association had a "come to Jesus" moment after Easter this year. I guess you never know where Jesus might show up after Easter.

Sometimes he shows up angry. It's true: Jesus is known for love, but love does not negate anger. Love is also persistent. It doesn't rest until the last lost sheep has been brought home to the fold. For only then will all be one.

The Sunday after Easter, Americans by the millions rose up in righteous anger to judge and condemn the owner of the Los Angeles Clippers as a vile racist. By Monday it appeared the NBA was on the verge of losing lots of respectability *and money*.

On that fateful Monday, players and fans spoke with one voice. Players would not play and fans would not show up unless that vile man was punished. Sponsors quickly disaffiliated from the team.

And thus at 2 o'clock Tuesday afternoon the commissioner of the NBA—with the full backing of players and every one of the 29 other team owners—judged, condemned, punished, and banished that errant owner for life.

And just like that the mood across America turned. One voice after another declared: *Today is a great day for America.* And it was.

I was one of many who couldn't wait to see how the players and fans would respond that evening. I stayed up late to see that historic moment live.

At last the moment arrived. The players jogged onto the floor of the Staples Center in LA while fans stood as one to applaud them *and a stunning moral victory for the NBA, its players, its fans, and by extension for the USA*. The arena was bedecked with signs declaring: WE ARE ONE.

A chill ran down my back and—much to my surprise—tears moistened my eyes. It was a moment to behold. It was a moment to remember a dream.

Imagine all the people
living life in peace
You may say I'm a dreamer,
but I'm not the only one.
I hope someday
you'll join us,
and the world will live
as one.
(John Lennon)

It was a moment of redemption. A moment to dream again. Even though most of the time we are fractured and fractious, we still hope.

We are one.

That evening in LA the voice of righteousness in our land was louder than the voice of wickedness. The NBA—along with millions of ordinary Americans—said with one voice: *Racism has no place in our nation, for we are one.*

Well, yes and no. Yes, we are one in more ways than one. But not completely so. After all, smugness creates divisions. You see, *We are one* is also a way of saying *You are not*. For the "we" in *We are one* includes only the righteous, namely, "us" on the inside and not "you" on the outside, *especially that vile one banished way out there in the wilderness!*

And that began to trouble me. I began to suspect something else going on beneath the jubilation. It's something we often see but don't always recognize.

That night in the Staples Center an ancient mythic ritual was at play.

In that cathartic moment countless hypocrites suddenly felt pretty good about themselves. Millions of Americans who blithely harbor racist attitudes toward people of color—*but have never been caught saying so out loud*—were breathing a sigh of relief and reveling in their piety. At last a scapegoat had been found and banished to the wilderness, carrying away our collective sins of racism.

That, in fact, is how the ancestors of my religious tradition got relief from guilt every year. They placed their collective sins on the head of one unfortunate goat that was then driven out into the wilderness to be devoured by wild beasts.

The scapegoat.

You can hear echoes of that ritual in the Christian tradition, which names Jesus as "the Lamb of God who takes away the sins of the world."

If only it were that easy.

It's not.

As the beloved and wise former NBA player Charles Barkley put it: *It will take more than the banishment of one NBA owner to banish racism from the heart and soul of our nation and its institutions.* And I would add: that includes our own hearts and souls, and the institutions we serve, such as our churches, schools, and the criminal justice system.

Pretending to be more righteous than we are keeps us above others. Getting off our high horse puts us on the level with others. And only then do we have a chance to become one with all. Despite a lifetime of effort, racism still lurks in my heart. So I keep at it, praying and working to vanquish it from my heart.

As Frederick Douglass put it: No struggle, no progress.

Redemption is not quick and easy. It's a long and sometimes tedious process of remorse, repentance, transformation, and making amends. We strive to live just, holy, and whole lives.

Nothing worth doing
can be achieved in our lifetime;
therefore we must be saved by hope.

Nothing which is true or beautiful or good
makes complete sense
in any immediate context of history;
therefore we must be saved by faith.

Nothing we do, however virtuous,
can be accomplished alone;
therefore we are saved by love.

No virtuous act is quite as virtuous
from the standpoint of our friend or foe
as it is from our own standpoint;

therefore we must be saved
by the final form of love,
which is forgiveness.
(Reinhold Niebuhr)

As it turns out, no one person—not even Messiah—no one singular act can redeem us once and for all. We must participate in the process of redemption. And that requires honesty, humility, and persistence.

It requires work.

We can do it.

And it's best done in the spirit of compassion and grace. ❧

STAY WITH US

Courage does not always roar. Sometimes courage is the quiet voice at the end of the day saying, "I will try again tomorrow."
— Mary Anne Radmacher

You can't keep picking people up.
You have to stop them from falling.
— Robin Williams,
Senate hearing on homelessness, May 9, 1990

The death of Robin Williams put suicide and mental illness on our minds and in our hearts, perhaps like never before. In case you hadn't heard or noticed, there is much mental illness in our country—by some estimates as many as one in four people suffer from mental illness—much of it misperceived and misunderstood.

Some mental illnesses are brain related and can be managed with medication. But some are environmental and social, related to personal, family, and community dynamics.

Not all mentally ill people take their own life or even contemplate doing so. And not every suicide is precipitated by mental illness. One explanation doesn't fit all.

In this world, many people are tormented by thoughts and feelings that push them to despair. It's tempting to shut our eyes and wish troubled people would go away. They disturb our tranquility—and sometimes our sleep.

In 1976 I took up residence in the Presbyterian manse on the corner of German and Church Streets. It was my first year as minister of Shepherdstown Presbyterian Church. And, as fate would have it, in that very first year, I was called to prevent a suicide.

The phone rang in the middle of the night. *Please, come quick,* cried the caller. *My friend is going to kill himself.* It was a neighbor whom I barely knew and who barely knew me.

I went to the apartment. I saw the young man with a pistol in his lap. I sat down and asked him what was going on.

He talked erratically. I listened. He said life no longer meant anything to him.

I told him people loved him and that he meant a lot to them. *These friends in this room, staying awake in the middle of the night with you, don't want you to check out.* But he could, I told him, take his life and we probably couldn't stop him, now or ever. *But,* I said, *we'd much, much rather you stay.*

It took hours, but eventually the dark spell passed. And as far as I know, he is still alive today.

The impulse for suicide in many cases passes fairly quickly. Yes, some of those who try once will try again. But most won't. Our job is to urge people to stay alive. We need them to stay with us. And they owe it to their "future self" to stay on.

A few years after that midnight visit in 1976, one of my own parishioners took his life. There was no midnight cry for help. No obvious foreshadowing. Only in hindsight could we see the signs.

He had been a U.S. Marine, a lieutenant in the Vietnam War. Intelligent beyond brilliance. Healthy and sound of mind, or so it seemed. But he left behind a wife and three young children. We mourned his death and celebrated his life at church. And then he was tenderly laid to rest in Elmwood Cemetery.

In another era he would have been denied a "Christian burial."

In some places, that's still the case. In some places suicide is considered a mortal sin, and the victims and their families are stigmatized, punished, and condemned.

But people who take their own lives should not be condemned or demonized after the fact. Nor should suicide be romanticized or glorified as some philosophers and poets have done. For suicide leaves an irreplaceable hole in the beautiful fabric of the world and the community in which the deceased once lived.

This past July, Sarah, age 47, a child of this town, also brilliant and radiant, full of promise, took her life after multiple attempts over 10 years. Mental illness and addiction darkened her mind.

In August, Ben, age 32, another child of this town, took his life at the Rumsey Monument. And then two days later, so did Robin Williams, one of the most joyous personalities we've ever seen.

All of that prompted me to read Jennifer Michael Hecht's book *Stay: A History of Suicide and Philosophies Against It.*

All suicides are not equal. Some who hasten the inevitable by their own hand have done so as a form of end-of-life management, not out of despair over life's futility. Hecht carefully distinguishes between those two kinds of suicide.

It's for those like Robin Williams and Sarah and young people like Ben that she writes, hoping that, despite the darkness in which such people live, they may hear real voices saying: *Stay. We need you. We love you. You are part of our community.*

Depression, of course, is no trifling matter. Yes, for some it is like a cold that will pass, but for most it is like cancer that won't go away. We owe it to such troubled souls to muster mental health resources that can give them a chance, the way we muster resources to give those with cancer or heart disease a chance.

(By the way, wouldn't it be better if our nation spent less on finding ways to kill people and more on finding ways to heal people?)

Hecht's book surveys changing attitudes toward suicide. In the Greek and Roman cultures, suicide was considered honorable in some cases; those who took their lives were even celebrated in art and literature, people such as the Roman woman Lucretia and the Greek philosopher Socrates.

The church itself took root within the Roman culture and initially accepted suicide, in part, because Jesus' death was seen as a kind of suicide, based on his words: *I take up my life and I lay it down of my own will. No one can take it from me.* (John 10:18)

But that attitude would change.

By the fourth century, the church would condemn suicide as murder, a violation of God's commandment against murder and against stealing, robbing God of what belonged only to God. The church assigned suicides to the deepest parts of hell, even publicly mutilating and displaying their bodies as a deterrent to others who might consider such a thing.

But that would change, too.

In modern culture, threats of God or hell are less successful as deterrents, which prompted Hecht to write *Stay* and offer secular reasons against suicide.

Over the past hundred years, we have come to better understand the nature of mental illness and the limits of human freedom and willpower. Hecht, along with others, I believe, sometimes overrates the powers of the mind and will, as if everyone can calmly and objectively answer the question *To be or not to be* and then do what the mind says. It's just not that simple or easy for many.

And so, when all is said and done, it is wise and compassionate to stand with the Buddha, who said: *Always assume people are doing the best they can with what they have to deal. For no one really knows. No one knows.*

And so to condemn those who give up on life is to arrogantly assume to know more than we do. And to give up on ourselves or others is to arrogantly assume to know more than we do about the future.

So we don't give up.

We don't give up on people while they are alive because we don't know what they still might be able to do. They may, in fact, have more courage and more reasons to live than they realize. It just might take a little time for them to see it.

The same courage and determination to end one's life may—just may!—be used to face the darkness and to live on. That too takes courage, and it inspires others to stay on.

Dark times are sure to come as sure as night follows day. But if we listen in the dark, we just might hear the Beloved saying to us and to those we love: *You are mine. Now and always you are mine. I hope you will stay. But if you can't, I will understand. For I love you and always will.*

But I'm pretty sure no one will hear that voice unless it comes from someone like you. ❧

SPRING 2015

REEFER MADNESS

Why does the government give our children the impression that alcohol is a safer choice than marijuana *when clearly it is not*?

Three years ago my son was arrested for possession and distribution of marijuana. He served time in federal prison. He deserved it, I figured, because he broke the law, and the law is always right. Or so I thought.

At that time I knew very little about the criminalization and demonization of marijuana. But I began reading books and reports and listening to law enforcement agents and health professionals, and I have come to believe that *marijuana should be legalized, controlled, and taxed the same way alcohol is.*

Six million Americans are in prison or under probation! More than half were convicted of nonviolent drug-related offenses. In most cases the drug is marijuana, and most of the inmates are young black men. (See *The New Jim Crow,* by Michelle Alexander.) The prison industry is booming and state budgets are breaking.

According to the Bible (Psalm 104), *God gives us bread to make us strong and wine to make our hearts glad*. For thousands of years, wine and cannabis—which is the proper name for marijuana—have relaxed many a body and made many a heart glad. Cannabis, like wine, also has many well-known therapeutic effects. But that's a different argument for legalization.

Take a little wine for the stomach's sake, the Apostle Paul advised his young friend Timothy. That's in the Bible. But so is this: *Do not be drunk with wine.*

Certain people should never ever again take a sip of alcohol. They are alcoholics, and the consequences of their drinking are dire.

Certain people should never ever again take a hit of pot. They are hooked, and their continual use of pot will do them great cognitive and emotional harm.

Millions partake of both of those drugs, and about 10 percent will become addicted. They are sick and need help. *It's a serious health issue but it isn't a crime.*

Still, there are many people who can drink alcohol or smoke pot with little negative effect; they do good work and never do harm to children or others. At least 200 million Americans use these drugs regularly and safely.

The three most popular nonprescription drugs are alcohol, tobacco, and marijuana. Each is harmful to the body and each creates social problems. Of the three, alcohol and tobacco are *proven* killers. Of those two, tobacco kills only its user (although secondhand smoke is no minor health hazard to others).

Tobacco does not fuel violence toward others.

Nor does pot.

Only alcohol does.

Two popular relaxants—alcohol and pot. You might wish that they weren't available or that neither was ever used, but *prohibition of alcohol is not coming back! Nor is universal abstinence likely to break out.*

Ask almost any law enforcement agent or health professional which drug creates the most mayhem in society, which destroys more brains, more lives, and more families, which turns people violent, crazy, out of control, and guess which drug will be named?

It's hardly a secret!

Those who abuse alcohol die by the thousands, including many young people. Why? Because with millions of dollars for propaganda and billions to be made, the beer industry has romanticized and glorified alcohol consumption, especially for college students. It's a virtual patriotic rite of passage to get drunk as a skunk!

On many campuses if you get caught drunk, your wrist will be slapped. Get caught stoned, and you could lose your scholarship or student loan, be kicked off the football team, or go to prison. And good luck finding a job after that.

Every year thousands of adults and hundreds of students die from overdosing on alcohol.

No one has ever died from an overdose of pot.

No one. Ever.

Still, *pot is not entirely safe*. Children and youth should never use it, just as they should never use tobacco or alcohol. The American Psychological Association and the American Medical Association have published warnings that cognitive and neurological damage from early pot use is comparable to that from early alcohol use.

Both pot and alcohol can be harmful if misused or abused. And yet only one is illegal.

Pot isn't illegal because it's more dangerous than alcohol. It's dangerous because it's illegal. Drug dealers never ask to see an ID. And many drug dealers have more than pot in their pocket. Even so, alcohol, as it turns out, is a far busier gateway to other drugs than pot is. And yet alcohol is still legal!

Soon after Prohibition was repealed in 1933 and Americans could legally buy the "devil's brew" again, something happened. Harry Anslinger, chief of the Federal Bureau of Narcotics, proclaimed—*without any medical or scientific support*—that pot was the "devil's weed," a drug that drove users to rape and kill. He made it clear that this was a scourge mostly among Hispanics and blacks.

Instead of "cannabis," the drug was now officially referred to as "marijuana" to associate it with Mexican farm workers in Texas. At that time William Randolph Hearst allegedly had financial and racist reasons to vilify Mexicans and cannabis. His nationwide chain of newspapers published lurid stories of murder and rape fueled by pot. It created national hysteria inflamed, in part, by the propaganda film *Reefer Madness.* Each state rushed to criminalize marijuana.

In 1972 the National Commission on Marijuana and Drug Abuse, headed by Republican Gov. Raymond Shafer of Pennsylvania, studied all the available evidence on marijuana and concluded: *Looking only at the effects on the individual, there is little proven danger of physical or psychological harm from the experimental or intermittent use of the natural preparations of cannabis.*

That report was rejected by President Richard Nixon, who was convinced that Vietnam War protesters were crazed by pot supplied by communists. He wanted hippies sent to jail. And thus began the "War on Drugs," the militarization of police forces, the packing of prisons, and the terrorizing of otherwise law-abiding Americans.

During this "war," 40 to 50 million Americans have continued to smoke pot. Why? Because they see through the government's lies.

Since 1965 more than 20 million citizens have been arrested for possession. Not all went to prison, of course. But nearly all of them had their lives ruined in one way or another, and nearly all live under constant dread of rearrest and imprisonment.

We are a nation of laws. I do not advocate breaking this law. I advocate changing it so that our children and our grandchildren will have a chance, a *real* chance to know the truth, the *real* truth, about the *real* dangers of *both* alcohol and cannabis, and so that adults in our nation can have the *legal* right to choose—as they once did—the one that is *really* far safer. ❧

QUESTION AUTHORITY!

(Really? Why should I?)

A Message To The Class of 2015

I
have
learned
so much from God
that I can no longer
call
myself
a Christian, a Hindu, a Muslim
a Buddhist, a Jew.
The Truth has shared so much of Itself
With me
That I can no longer call myself
A man, a woman, an angel,
Or even pure
Soul.
Love has
Befriended Hafiz so completely
It has turned to ash
And freed
Me
Of every concept and image
My mind has ever known.
— Hafiz
14th-century Persian Sufi Muslim

~

I graduated from high school 50 years ago. That would be 1965.

In 1965 the first Ford Mustang officially rolled out. In 1965 we were dancing to the Beatles, the Rolling Stones, Elvis, and Chubby Checker. We could twist and shout and shimmy under the limbo stick.

The United States was about to launch manned rockets into space on the way to a moon landing in 1969. It was a time of great optimism. We trusted and respected authority.

And then the roof fell in.

Our nation lost its way in Vietnam and couldn't get out without destroying half that beautiful country and killing a million civilians, including children. We went in to stop communist aggression only to find that the Vietnamese people considered us the aggressor.

Within a couple of years fewer and fewer Americans could answer the questions: *What are we fighting for? What in the world are we doing way over there, spending billions of dollars and losing thousands of young American lives when there's plenty to take care of right here at home?*

There may be times when there are good reasons to be "way over there." But never be too sure. I hope you and your generation will keep asking that question: *What in the world are we doing?*

In 1968 Martin Luther King was assassinated. Cities erupted in riots and burst into flames. The lid pressed down upon racial injustice in our society blew off. We suddenly learned the difference between tranquility and peace. We learned there could be no peace without justice. Tranquility, yes; peace, no.

Before you judge or condemn so-called rioters, I hope you will walk a mile in their shoes or, better yet, imagine living a year in their neighborhoods. And do the same for the police. Walk a mile in their shoes.

That's called empathy. It's a form of love and it requires deep listening.

1965 was a time of great optimism in our country. We trusted and respected authority.

And then the roof fell in.

My generation began to question authority. That bumper sticker (QUESTION AUTHORITY) was everywhere. I began questioning what I had been taught about Jesus and Christianity.

I don't know if you're a Christian. But if you are, I'm pretty sure "Christian" is not part of your Facebook profile or something you want tattooed on your forehead. I'm guessing you're more ashamed than proud to be a Christian. And considering what goes for Christianity in our society, I don't blame you.

According to a recent survey, when young people like you are asked to identify as Christian, Jew, Muslim, Hindu, Buddhist, or None of the Above, more and more of them check None. Hence the recent headline: *Rise of the Nones.*

And that's a good thing. I'd much rather someone else call you a Christian than you call yourself one. "Christian" is a far better adjective than a noun. And since you are a high school graduate, I know you know the difference.

If you were ever baptized, which is to say, initiated into the Christian tradition and if you should ever be outed, I hope you can claim that identity humbly without apology. There are reasons for shame. But there are reasons for pride as well.

St. Francis is one. Mother Teresa is another. And, of course, Martin Luther King is yet another. He was—in case you didn't hear it in school—a baptized child of the church.

And by the way, it's far more important to live like Christ than to call yourself a Christian. Being a Christian isn't so much about what you believe as it is about what you practice.

Despite the many names of religions in this world, there are really only two: the religion of *being right* and the religion of *being kind*. It doesn't have to be either-or, but if you can manage only one, please, *be kind*.

When I questioned authority, I discovered I had been misled about Jesus. I had been told that Jesus is the only way to heaven because he said: "In my Father's house are many mansions. I am the way, the truth and the life. No one comes to the Father but by me."

I don't know what you'll learn over the 50 years after you graduate, but one thing I learned was that when you take the Bible seriously, you don't take it all literally. "The Father," as it turns out, is a poetic symbol. It represents our true home, where we belong. That doesn't mean some other realm beyond this world. It is right here.

Heaven is what we make or experience here on earth. "Heaven" is a better adjective than a noun. And the same goes for "hell."

As the Bible puts it elsewhere: *Those who abide in love abide in God.* So when you connect the dots, "in my Father's house are many mansions" can mean there is plenty of room for love in this world. There are many ways and opportunities to love others.

In the gospels, "Jesus" stands for love. The way of Jesus is the way of love. So you see, Christianity itself isn't the way, the truth, and the life. Love is. Love is the way, the truth, and the life. No matter the religion—love is the way.

Whether you call yourself a Christian or not, I hope you will bear the light of love into your world as St. Francis did in his day. Francis set aside the luxuries and privileges of his highborn life in order to serve the poor, the sick, and the hungry in his society. After serving as a warrior in his youth, he gave up the sword and adopted the way of love. During a 13th-century crusade when Christians and Muslims were at war, he visited the sultan in Egypt several times in order to find a way toward peace.

I don't know what job or career you will take up. I hope it will be a good one, constructive, challenging, wholesome, and with decent pay and benefits. You may have many jobs in your lifetime. But ultimately, you have only one vocation. It is your calling as a human being to *wholeheartedly* love the One and all others, including the earth and all that dwells therein.

The late, great B.B. King once told a workshop of budding musicians who apparently idolized him (and why not?): "It's good to have idols and mentors. But the world doesn't need another B.B. King. The world needs you to be you."

To which I would add: The world doesn't need another St. Francis, Mother Teresa, Martin Luther King, or even another Jesus. The world needs you to be you—full of joy, full of faithfulness, full of hope, full of love, which is to say, the world needs you to be fully alive. ❧

FALL 2015

DRUG ALERT

Pot, Porn, & Fox News

Be careful how you live, not as unwise people but as wise, making the most of the time, because the days are evil.
— EPHESIANS 5:15–16

Are these evil days?

Parents think so.

Pot, heroin, and pornography are readily available everywhere.

Every parent I know is worried.

And it's not just children and youth that are vulnerable. We all are.

But as dangerous and destructive as drugs and porn can be, there is another evil out and about that is hurting our people and our nation. It's called "fear mongering," and it, too, is *a highly intoxicating, addictive, dangerous, and destructive drug.*

And it's readily available on Fox News. If you don't think the world is evil, just watch Fox and you'll see.

When I tell my friends that I watch Fox News they cringe, because "friends don't let friends watch that network." But I watch it anyway, because I want to understand how others see the world. I want to know why they think the way they do. Maybe they know something I don't. It doesn't hurt to be humble.

And so I watch and listen. I want to be open—but that doesn't mean I surrender my values or convictions.

For the past several years I have watched Fox News religiously, and boy, oh boy, talk about evil—four of the five pundits on "The Five" at 5 o'clock see evil everywhere *all the time*. And from what I've heard, the prime-time pundits are not much different. The world in their eyes is a grim and scary place.

For example, they see our president's deal with Iran as leading Israelis to the "oven doors." And if that ain't evil, what is?

They see a despicable criminal, a "traitor" to our nation about to become the Democratic presidential nominee. And if that ain't evil, what is?

They see the "Black Lives Matter" movement as a ploy to stir up racial animosity in this country, where racism hardly even exists anymore.

They see gay rights as infringing on religious freedoms.

They see Planned Parenthood auctioning off fetal parts for profit.

They see illegal immigrants hauling drugs and diseases into our country and raping our daughters.

And they see radical Islamic terrorist cells in nearly every American city about to attack a mall, a school, or a church near you, and they think our president is too wimpy, too spineless, and too un-American to name or confront that threat.

Be afraid, people. Be very, very afraid.

Yes, these pundits are scary but they are not evil. In fact, they can be civil, rational, kind, and even humorous at times. But then it's right back to doom and gloom, fear, and more fear.

One fear is a gateway to another and another.

In case you hadn't heard, fearful people will turn on each other, surrender rights, and gleefully applaud the death of enemies. And if that ain't evil, what is?

If I didn't know better or didn't have other sources of information, I'd be terrified and angry all the time. I'd want to take this country back! *Please, somebody, anybody, get rid of all this evil and make America great again!*

If I didn't know better, I'd want us to bomb Iran *right now*—and possibly half of Syria and northern Iraq on the way over. And I'd not rule out nuclear weapons, *if that's what it takes to destroy ISIS*.

If I didn't know better, I'd get a gun and be ready to shoot anyone who looks Muslim or Mexican.

If I didn't know better, I'd think white men were the real victims in our society.

Be afraid, white people. Be very, very afraid.

Many people watch and listen. Many think they're getting fair and balanced reporting. But what they're really getting is hooked. One fear is a gateway to another and another and another. Fear, after all, is a rush, a kind of high.

Many good and decent people see all this differently. But what I see is this: a well-funded, mean-spirited, concerted effort—from Fox News and other sources in our nation—to misrepresent reality in order to undermine the great American vision, the great experiment of unity with great diversity (*e pluribus unum*); to forsake the way of cooperation for the way of belligerence; to forsake democracy for oligarchy.

These are smart and sincere people. But smart and sincere is not enough.

As we learned to say after the catastrophic invasion of Iraq in 2003: *so much intelligence; so little wisdom*.

Just because you're smart doesn't mean you're wise.

To be wise, in part, means to listen to those with whom we disagree, to give them the benefit of the doubt we'd like for ourselves. And so I have, religiously, for more than two years.

And I've learned again and again: We don't all see the world the same way.

Some see evil and terror around every corner. Others see goodness and grace. Some foment fear and hate. Others promote hope and love. In fact, sometimes I'm one sort; sometimes I'm another.

These are troubling times—troubling times for our youth tempted by drugs and troubling times for our nation and others tempted to buy the seductive drugs of fear and violence.

We don't have to resign ourselves to fatalism or succumb to fear. We can seek wisdom and courage—wisdom to understand the way of love and courage to undertake it with all our hearts.

Yes, there is much grim news in the world. But there is also great joy.

Take joy. ❧

WINTER 2015

LOVE YOUR ENEMY

Kill ISIS

~

We are scared to death.

We now know that the angry, hateful, crazed, and ruthless agents of the fundamentalist militant Islamic group known as ISIS can wreak death and destruction just about anywhere. If they can randomly slaughter defenseless civilians in the heart of Paris, they can strike a restaurant, movie theatre, stadium, or concert hall near you—or your next flight.

There is no safe place.

Terror strikes fear in our hearts. We can't control our reaction. But we can control our response.

Breathe in love. Breathe out fear.

We must not allow fear to destroy our nation more completely than a terrorist attack ever could. To divide our nation or the world into Us against Them is to invite disaster. Such pathological dualism fuels ISIS's "holy war."

We must not succumb to pathological dualism. We are Them. And They are Us.

Every person is capable of great good and great evil. And every nation is capable of great good and great evil. To think otherwise is naive and delusional. Like it or not, we are all one family. We are more akin than we may admit.

Democrats and Republicans, Sunnis and Shias need to take a deep breath and remember that love is more powerful than hate. That doesn't mean we should allow murderous thugs to kill us or our loved ones. To love your enemies doesn't mean to let them trample over you. It does, however, mean to regard them as brothers or sisters gone mad.

If my brother came to kill my children and I could only stop him with a bullet, I would. I would protect my children fiercely. But I would not gloat if my bullet killed my brother. I would cry my eyes out. I would feel deep regret and remorse and eventually ask myself: *What did I and our parents do to contribute to his rage and madness?* We'd have to examine family history.

What did the West do to contribute to ISIS's rage and madness? We have to examine family history. But first, ISIS must be destroyed. Our nation along with the nations of Europe and the Middle East must rally to stop it from committing more vicious, cold-blooded murders.

Military force can stop it. That's what our troops are trained to do. War can bring peace for a spell. But only for a spell. It's a first step. It provides time and space to establish political solutions.

Violence can destroy ISIS. But violence can't destroy its toxic ideology. Nor can its adherents be assuaged with the comforts and pleasures of mere materialism. They are fighting to remake the world, not to own a Fiat or a flat-screen TV.

Is there a universal vision in the heart of humankind more compelling and inspiring than their sectarian caliphate? I think there is. But it can't be delivered on the point of a sword. It must be conveyed by words and demonstrated by actions.

Universal kinship is the vision that leads to a new world. Love is more powerful than hate; reconciliation more powerful than retaliation. Hearts of stone can be transformed.

I recently revisited the Great Ancestors' mythic tale of Cain and Abel, the first brothers. Cain thought Abel was favored. Cain felt mistreated.

Many people, groups, and nations know that feeling. The world seems to favor some over others.

Cain was hurt and angry. And so he killed his brother in cold blood.

What if Abel had seen it coming? What if Abel had intelligence that warned him? What if he had packed a knife? What if he had struck first and killed Cain? Would Abel have rejoiced? Would he not have felt regret and even remorse and eventually asked questions of himself, his parents, and their family history?

Cain could not overcome sibling rivalry and hatred. Still, God did not reject Cain. God provided a way for him to come home, to come to his senses. "God," in this ancient tale, is more a parent than a judge.

According to legend, Abraham's son Isaac, born of Sarah, is the father of the Jewish people. Ishmael, his half brother, born of Hagar, is the father of Muslims.

Each had reason to hate the other. Each thought the other more favored. They grew apart. But when their father, Abraham, died, they stood side by side at his grave, reconciled. They had found their way home. Brothers in love.

This looks like the story of one family, but as it turns out, it is a narrative about all families, tribes, and nations. We may be one family, but we are all capable of hating and killing each other if anger gets the best of us. Real or perceived injustice against us or our loved ones ignites our anger.

Anger is a healthy reaction to injustice. We can't control our reaction. But we can control our response.

And that's where faith comes in. Love is more powerful than hate. There is always a way back home, a way toward reconciliation. So all you need is love! Right? No, not really.

Love is great. But love is not enough, for love plays favorites. Love is particular.

Something else is needed, something more universal. And that's where justice comes in. For justice is the social and political expression of love. *What does the Lord require of us but to love kindness, do justice, and walk humbly.* (Micah 6:8)

We walk humbly knowing that even our enemy is truly our brother or sister. It may be virtually impossible to empathize with ISIS, to stand in their boots for even a second, but love requires the effort. Even Cain won God's sympathy and grace.

"Love your enemy" is not a platitude or sentimentality. It is a practice that requires a change of heart. Conversion. It takes courage. And it takes faith.

It takes faith and courage to overcome endless cycles of retaliation and revenge. It takes faith and courage to overcome tribal and national hostility with a vision of universal kinship. We are all children in one great and diverse family. We look, think, and pray differently, but we are all kin.

Still, we must keep armed forces and police forces ready. We hang on to our swords. But we hold them sadly and reluctantly until the day when all swords will be turned into pruning hooks and none shall study war anymore.

In his book *Not in God's Name: Confronting Religious Violence*, Rabbi Jonathan Sacks tells the following story.

On Friday January 9, 2015, two days after the attack on the offices of the French newspaper *Charlie Hebdo*, an Islamist terrorist entered a kosher supermarket in Paris and killed four Jews. A Muslim employee, Lassana Bathily, saw what was happening and, out of sight of the gunman, hid 20 Jewish customers in a cold-storage room, saving their lives.

When he was later commended for his courage, Lassana replied: "We are all brothers and sisters. It's not a question of Jews, Christians, or Muslims. We were all in the same boat. We had to help each other get out of the crisis."

And maybe that's why the French are still willing to accept 30,000 Muslim Syrian refugees. It may be humane but it is also rational. If only our own nation could be as rational.

Of course, there could be a terrorist lurking among those 30,000. But more likely there are hundreds, perhaps thousands, of Lassanas, one or more of whom may someday thwart a catastrophic terrorist attack and save French lives again.

We are all brothers and sisters. It's not a question of Jews, Christians, or Muslims. We are all in the same boat. We have to help each other get out of the crisis. ❧

SPRING 2016

FAN MAIL

Last September I received an angry letter in response to my essay "Drug Alert: Pot, Porn, and Fox News," in which I denounced that news outlet for fear mongering. The writer said I was *vicious, hateful, rude, self-righteous, arrogant, divisive, condescending, liberal, snide, sophomoric* (that hurt!), *and a disgrace to the name of Christ*. And that was just the first page.

The letter was signed: *Yours, in Christ*. There was no signature, nothing to identify the writer. Still, that letter made my day. I love fan mail.

The writer sent a copy of that letter to every minister in town, just in case my colleagues didn't already know those things about me. I don't resent the criticism one bit. I only wish the writer had included contact information, because I would like to respond to him or her as I did to the other dozen or so people who called or emailed me with complaints, admonitions, and rebukes.

I'd like to commend the writer for being so perceptive. I really and truly am *vicious, hateful, rude, self-righteous, arrogant, divisive, condescending, liberal, snide, sophomoric, and a disgrace to the name of Christ*. Not all the time, but certainly some of the time. And I suspect that particular essay might have been one of those times.

I was hoping nobody would notice. But obviously some did, and they were kind enough to let me know, in most cases because they truly care about me and my reputation as a bridge builder.

"Why must you take sides?" several asked.

I thanked each person for helping me see things more clearly and helping me understand myself a little better. After all, there's always more than one way to say something—some kinder than others. As the Buddhists put it, *It's OK to announce, but don't denounce, for denouncing is a form of violence.* Or, as the Apostle Paul put it, *Speak the truth in love.*

In this case anger got the best of me. The relentless litany of woe and negativity on one particular news show over a six-month period enraged me. Sure, it's OK to be angry. But it's not OK for anger to get the best of us.

Just as I was finishing that essay, I realized my own hypocrisy and negativity. And so I inserted a parenthetical confession of sorts near the end: "Some foment fear and hate. Others promote hope and love. In fact, sometimes I'm one sort; sometimes I'm another." But many readers—blinded by anger over the "Pot, Porn, and Fox News" headline—never got to the confession or simply missed it.

As fate would have it, the day before that blistering letter arrived, I had been reading the Vietnamese Buddhist monk Thich Nhat Hanh's classic *Being Peace,* in which he says, "If we align ourselves with one side or the other, we will lose our chance to work for peace." And then he says, "Be peace, don't just talk about it."

Be peace before you try to *make* peace. Breathe in peace; breathe out fear. Breathe in love; breathe out hatred and bigotry.

"If in our daily life we can smile, if we can be peaceful and happy, not only we, but everyone, will profit from it. This is the most basic kind of peace work. Breathe in calm; breathe out smiles."

The day before that letter arrived I was also reading this gospel story: *Once upon a time the disciples spoke sternly to those who tried to bring children to Jesus.* Jesus, just like us, had much more important things to do, or so the disciples thought. But Jesus said: *Let the little children come to me; do not stop them.*

Breathe in calm; breathe out smiles.

I'm guessing Jesus knew what the Buddha knew. Breathe in calm and breathe out smiles. I'm guessing Jesus was smiling when he blessed the little children. A scowling Jesus would have sent the children flying.

That little gospel episode isn't just about children. It's a lesson in acceptance as taught in *Being Peace*. It's about inviting that which can be annoying, irritating, or interrupting of our well-guarded lives.

Be careful, say the Buddhists, about rejecting things you don't like or don't want in your life. Learn to accept and if possible embrace them. Embrace darkness, embrace suffering, embrace criticism—and let it be. For darkness and suffering are our teachers, too.

And so I thank my anonymous critic for bringing me back to my senses and to deep breathing. Breathe in calm. Breathe out smiles.

And so here's a smile coming your way, my friend: Yours, in Christ. Which is to say, *Yours, in Love.* ❧

SUMMER 2016

A WHOLESOME TABLE

In the presence of my enemies

Recently, I reread Psalm 23 ("The Lord is My Shepherd") in light of what I've been learning about nutrition. *You prepare a table before me in the presence of my enemies*. Indeed, many enemies are aligned against our health. And we may be our own worst enemy. The American diet is slowly killing us.

But we are not doomed. We can choose another way of eating.

Full disclosure: I am no paragon of healthy eating. I occasionally crave a Big Mac or fish and chips washed down with a Guinness, which, if you can believe the Irish, is "as good as milk." Which begs the question: *And how GOOD is milk?*

Anyway, I may not always practice what I preach, but truth must still be preached and that includes the truth about food. Eating, as it turns out, is as much a spiritual practice as prayer and charity. If our bodies are "temples" of the Holy One, they must be respected and protected.

I was blessed to have a mother who prepared a wholesome table. She fed her family from a garden of tomatoes, beans, lettuce, radishes, onions, and corn. She believed in eating lots of vegetables and fruit. But she eventually succumbed to the convenience of processed foods and their time-saving benefits as touted by advertisements. And so we occasionally ate fish sticks and tater tots.

She also believed the government's food pyramid, not knowing it was influenced by Big Agriculture, Big Beef, and Big Dairy. So we ate lots of meat and eggs and drank lots of milk to make our bones strong. Over and over she was told: *Milk is good for every body.* And: *You can't get protein without meat.*

But we've now learned that ain't so. We are wising up.

The dramatic increase in cancer, diabetes, heart disease, and obesity since World War II is no fluke. It can easily be traced to a change in the American diet. We are a nation of ever more sick and sickly people.

The food industry, like the tobacco industry, has foisted misleading information upon us. Even package labeling is designed to confuse. We throw up our hands in frustration. Who has time and patience to sort it all out? Besides, next year they'll tell us what was bad for us is now good.

My wife sets a table that's even more wholesome than my mother's. But on road trips with our children, I'm ashamed to admit, we frequently stopped at the Golden Arches. It was convenient and cheap—*and the bathrooms were clean!*

A few years ago we were on a road trip with our New Mexico granddaughters, who were four years old at the time. In Carlsbad we nonchalantly pulled into a McDonald's. At the sight of the Golden Arches both screamed at once: NO! NOT MCDONALD'S! YUCK! YUCK! IT'S POISON!

That's what I call progress.

We are learning to eat better. Local farming and farmers markets help.

Shopping and eating habits are hard to break. But if we can't break them, don't worry. Another Big is ready to help make it easy on us. If an unwholesome diet makes us sick or sickly, Big Pharma will save us.

Got a health problem? No worries. We'll make a pill to fix it. Can't eat wholesome foods? No worries. We'll make a nutritional supplement.

Everybody seems to be working on ways to cure cancer, heart disease, diabetes, and obesity; not so many on ways to prevent them. Follow the money—billions to research cures and manufacture pills for this and that; pennies to teach and promote prevention.

So let me add my two cents: *Wholesome eating fortifies health and prevents most diseases. Food, after all, is the best medicine.*

Lately I've been feasting on books about nutrition: *Whole: Rethinking the Science of Nutrition*, by Colin Campbell; *Healthy Eating, Healthy World: Unleashing the Power of Plant-Based Nutrition*, by J. Morris Hicks; and *Food Revolution*, by John Robbins.

I have also seen the film *Forks Over Knives*, which makes the case that if we put healthier food on our *forks*, we wouldn't have to go under the *knife* for heart and artery repairs nearly as often, if at all. Think about it. Which is more *radical* behavior: to eat mainly fruits, vegetables, grains, rice, and beans with little or no meat or to have your chest cut open and arteries patched?

That shouldn't be a hard choice to make.

A friend who suffered with high blood pressure and signs of heart disease switched to a whole-food, plant-based diet three years ago and now is off a dozen medications and down 30 pounds. I've also heard of diabetics who reversed and even eliminated their condition on such a nutritional plan.

According to John Robbins, a "food revolution" is coming much like the revolution that dramatically changed society's attitude and behavior toward tobacco. The food revolution is moving rather quickly. It is led by lots of millennials, a cohort with huge influence in the marketplace. From what I've read, 30 percent of millennials are vegetarians compared with 3 percent of the general population. Grocery stores and restaurants are adapting, including several in Shepherdstown.

These millennials haven't changed their habits just for their own health, eating lower on the food chain to reduce the risk of obesity, diabetes, heart disease, and cancer. They eat that way because they have also heard this shocking news: *The skyrocketing worldwide demand for meat is killing the planet.*

The increase in air pollution and global warming can be traced in large part to the destruction of more and more rainforest to raise more and more grain to fatten more and more cattle to satisfy the world's demand for more and more meat. And that demand has also forced countless cattle, chickens, and pigs into farm factories where they never see the light of day, peck insects from the soil, or munch on grass.

The local food movement has certainly brought about some humane alternative to the industrialization of animals. And yet far too many sentient beings, our fellow animals, our planetary friends are cruelly mistreated. Future generations will look back and ask: *What were you thinking?*

But we don't have to wait. We can ask that question of ourselves now. And we can modify our diet.

I can't recommend a full vegetarian or vegan diet for everybody. But I can recommend awareness, compassion, and wisdom. The first step is to get informed. Here are some good places to start: forksoverknives.com, nutritionstudies.org, and foodrevolution.org.

We and the whole planet, including our fellow animals, would all be better off if we prepared a holy and wholesome table for ourselves. ❧

THE FIRE NEXT TIME

God gave Noah the rainbow sign
no more water—the fire next time.
— Negro spiritual

I came to bring fire to the earth,
and how I wish it were already kindled!
— Jesus of Nazareth (Luke 12:49–56)

Rage is burning like fire across our nation and around the world. The scorned and forgotten of our nation rage against a smug, self-serving establishment. Black Lives Matter rages against the police and the police fire back. ISIS rages against a certain world smug in its privilege, power, prosperity, and heresies. And that world fires back.

Bombs explode in cars, and bodies are torn apart.

Bombs fall from the sky, and bodies are torn apart.

Bombs explode in presidential campaign rhetoric. National and racial unity is torn apart.

Rage is burning like fire across our nation and around the world.

Anger is like fire. It can destroy or it can create. It all depends.

According to the Greek myth, Prometheus sneaked behind Zeus's back to give mortals the gift of fire. For that Prometheus was forever tortured by Zeus. Zeus did not want mortals to have the power to remake the world or themselves. But it was too late. We got it. Fire in our hands. Fire in our imaginations.

Fire seethes in many hearts today, a fire of frustration with so much injustice, stupidity, bigotry, and willful ignorance in our land. Anger isn't bad. Anger is a healthy reaction to such things. Anger is a healthy reaction to real or perceived injustice against ourselves or those we love.

Anger is like fire. It can create or it can destroy. It can be constructive or it can be destructive. It all depends.

That fire burning in many souls today is like the fire that burned in the souls of enslaved Africans. You can hear it in their song: *God gave Noah the rainbow sign / no more water—the fire next time.* That Negro spiritual inspired James Baldwin's 1963 book, *The Fire Next Time.*

In that book Baldwin laments and indicts a so-called Christian nation for its hypocrisy in denying complicity in the torture and oppression of the black race. How can you miss the "lynching trees"? How can you not see that as terrorism? Christians, of all people, should have known better. But most were willfully blind.

You hypocrites! cried Jesus, *You know how to forecast the weather and interpret the appearance of earth and sky, but why do you not know how to interpret the present time?*

Does anybody know what time it is? Does anybody understand these times?

Which is to say: You are so smart. You are so well educated. You are so savvy. So why, then, can't you see what's going on right under your nose? As Bob Dylan put in "Subterranean Homesick Blues," *You don't need to be a weatherman to know which way the wind blows.*

Do we know which way the wind is blowing? Does anybody understand these times? Can we see what's now been exposed in our nation?

In his time and place, Jesus was angry at the way things were. Love does not exclude anger. Anger, however, must be tempered by compassion lest it become hurtful and destructive.

Even "God," according to the Great Ancestors, had to learn that lesson.

Once upon a time, God got angry at the way things were and sent a universal flood to wipe out all of humanity because God was disgusted with its violent and unjust ways. That story seems to locate "righteous anger" in a distant God above the earth. But there's another way of reading that mythic folktale.

In that story human anger and frustration are projected onto God. But that anger and disgust actually reflect our own frequent reactions to an unjust world. How many times have you felt like wiping out all the bad and evil people in the world, people like ISIS or perhaps your in-laws or your obnoxious neighbors, classmates, workmates, or that other political party? "I'd like to wipe them all out and start over with a few truly good folks like me."

The story of "The Flood" ends with a rainbow in the sky as if to say, enough of this raging, self-righteous anger. Violence cannot end violence. Another way must be found. According to that mythic tale, "God" learned a lesson, which is to say, mortals were beginning to learn that lesson. Untempered anger is destructive.

And certain partisans in our country had better learn that lesson soon.

God gave Noah the rainbow sign / no more water—the fire next time.

We can hear that fire in the voice of Jesus. *I came to bring fire to the earth, and how I wish it were already kindled! Do you think that I have come to bring peace to the earth? No, I tell you, not peace but rather division!*

Families, said Jesus, will be divided against themselves. How can that be the mission of the Prince of Peace, the advocate of love? How can division and conflict be good?

Well, it would not be good unless it separates families, tribes, and nations from blind loyalties that prevent them from embracing and practicing a higher and wider form of love—love of all, not just one's own family, race, tribe, or nation; love of one's enemies, not just our friends or our kind and kindred.

To embrace that vision and live it can and will cause divisions. It just will. The more the promise of universal love spreads, the more some people will feel threatened. They will resort to bigotry and fear mongering trying to hang on to their privileges and position, trying to preserve the old world and its sham unity.

If you embrace and practice universal kinship, not everyone will be on your side. At times you will have to stand your ground alone.

Not everything we call "peace" is peace. Peace without justice for the oppressed is no peace. Tranquility, maybe, but not peace. "Law and order" without justice, without healing, without reconciliation, and without compassion is not peace. It's a sham.

God gave Noah the rainbow sign / no more water—the fire next time.

Water and more water will never convert a lump of coal. Only fire can.

Hate and more hate will not transform a broken world. Only love can.

We can settle for tranquility, serenity, cordiality, and mere tolerance. And those aren't bad things. Or we can take the fire of love in our hearts and imaginations, go deeper, cleanse wounds, and heal divisions in the world, in our nation, in communities, and in our homes. It may not be easy but it will be worth it. ☙

NATIONAL CRISIS

Live into hope!

THE GATES OF HOPE

Our mission is to plant ourselves at the gates of Hope—
Not the prudent gates of Optimism,
Which are somewhat narrower.
Not the stalwart, boring gates of Common Sense;
Nor the strident gates of Self-Righteousness,
Which creak on shrill and angry hinges
(People cannot hear us there; they cannot pass through)
Nor the cheerful, flimsy garden gate of
"Everything is gonna be all right."

But a different, sometimes lonely place,
The place of truth-telling,
About your own soul first of all and its condition.
The place of resistance and defiance,
The piece of ground from which you see the world
Both as it is and as it could be
As it will be;
The place from which you glimpse not only struggle,
But the joy of the struggle.

And we stand there, beckoning and calling,
Telling people what we are seeing
Asking people what they see.
— Victoria Safford

One month later and many of my friends are still reeling in shock, anger, dismay, and even depression in the wake of the election. And for some it's getting worse, not better.

Nobody better tell them to "get over it." I mean, even if the angel of the Lord appeared and said, "Fear not; be not afraid," they'd still be afraid and think the appearance a hoax.

One day shortly after the election, while wandering outside my echo chamber, I stumbled upon some other friends, friends who were pleased, relieved, and even delighted with the election. Those weren't my feelings.

But since I know them to be good and honorable people, and since I don't know everything, and since I often prejudge and stereotype people, and since I (sometimes) practice what I preach, I asked why they felt pleased, relieved, and delighted. What did you see in *him* that I didn't?

I got an earful. And I'm pretty sure I got a glimpse of the world through their eyes.

That's what happens when *we plant ourselves at the gates of hope, telling people what we are seeing and asking them what they see.*

And so I asked.

Nobody knows the future. We can only guess. And some guesses make more sense than others. But we can't *know*. And yet we do know this: Right now, in this moment, our nation faces a crisis. And crisis spells both danger and opportunity.

And one opportunity is to listen to others and see the world as they see it. Empathy is a great virtue. It's an aspect of compassion, which, by the way, isn't the same thing as being nice.

As it turns out, much to my surprise, some of my good friends and kinfolk—along with 50 million others—saw "hope and change" where I had seen only vulgarity, vitriol, and bigotry. They didn't change my view, but they broadened my horizon.

In a broken world, no one sees clearly. That's why love requires not only kindness, justice, and humility but a willingness to listen carefully and deeply to others who see the world differently than we do, even if, in the end, we can't endorse their views.

One aspect of the Golden Rule is *Give others the same benefit of the doubt that you'd like for yourself.*

So I did.

The promise of "hope and change" is powerful. It gets a grip on people despite evidence and reason. Hope and optimism are not the same things. Optimism is based on evidence, trends, statistics; hope comes from a different place. And it's not exactly rational.

Yes, it could turn out to be false hope. And yet in the moment it's gladly embraced, because most people at most times desperately want hope.

As I listened to these (annoyingly) happy friends, I remembered that eight years ago, 70 million Americans were inspired by Senator Barack Obama's promise of "hope and change." Many of those 70 million overlooked his gross inexperience and voted *against* their own racial biases and partisan loyalties to elect America's first black president. They craved "hope and change."

Then as now, expectations soared to messianic heights. And not surprisingly, many people were disappointed.

In the wake of this election, we all have expectations in one direction or the other. I'm guessing many will be disappointed again—some gravely so. As the Buddha put it: "Only the one who has no expectations is never disappointed."

Our mission is to plant ourselves at the gates of Hope—
Not the prudent gates of Optimism,
Nor the cheerful, flimsy garden gate of
"Everything is gonna be all right."

Hope is not always cheerful. Hope does not ignore dark clouds. Yes, the sun comes up every day. But it's foolish and dangerous to ignore storm clouds on the other horizon.

At times such as these, it's good to take a deep breath and a long perspective. It's a good time to let the natural world teach us a few lessons.

Turbulence and turmoil keep this planet alive. Without hurricanes, tsunamis, monsoons, earthquakes, and raging forest fires, this planet would be cold dead. Life on planet earth is turbulent. It just is.

If you've lived long enough and paid attention, you know that personal and political worlds also shake, rattle, and collapse. Worlds collapse all the time. We mustn't take it personally, as though we alone suffer devastation.

Many poets and prophets have proclaimed: *Destruction can be the prelude to a new creation; sometimes something more beautiful and wholesome arises.*

Crisis spells danger and opportunity. This is no time for complacency.

This election opened our eyes to hordes of people living lives of quiet despair. One candidate saw them more clearly than the other.

But no matter our partisan loyalties, we must now devote ourselves again to abolishing bigotry, violence, misogyny, sexism, greed, racism, poverty, addiction, inequality, and elitism. We must live into hope.

Hope is hard. Life is hard. But something else is true: Grace abounds. And in hard times it helps to be gracious.

President-elect Donald Trump is a *real* winner! Obviously, he knows how to win. He likes a challenge, the bigger the better. He now faces the biggest challenge of his life.

And so I pray that the president-elect will be blessed with a heart and mind devoted to winning back the many he has wounded and terrified. It can be done. But despite his claims, he alone cannot fix it.

Whether he tries or not, whether he succeeds or not, we are all summoned to hard and holy work. Left, right, and center. We must now work together to mend divisions; tear down walls of hostility; build up the economy; protect women and girls, Muslims, immigrants, and LGBTQ people; and ensure that all Americans, not just some, can feel great about our country again.

No, I'm not a starry-eyed optimist. I see many reasons to be pessimistic. But I am hopeful, and I also happen to believe in the amazing power of love.

Now abideth faith, hope, and love. And the greatest of these is love. (1 Corinthians 13:13) ☙

SPRING 2017

TAKING SIDES

What does the Lord require of you but to do justice, love kindness,
and walk humbly with your God?
— The Prophet Micah

My one and only brother Jerry died nine years ago. He was eight years older than me. We lived in the same house, went to the same church, and read the same Bible. But we lived in different worlds. We fiercely disagreed on nearly everything. He was on one side. I was on another.

He loved Doris Day, Perry Como, and the Kingston Trio. I loved Janis Joplin, John Lennon, and the Rolling Stones. He supported the Vietnam War. I did not.

He thought Martin Luther King was a communist agitator. I thought King was a saint. He admired Richard Nixon. I admired Eugene McCarthy.

He loved Jerry Falwell. I thought Falwell was a satanic agitator. He was a proud fundamentalist. I am not. He read the Bible literally. I do not.

My brother regularly read my essays here in the *Good News Paper* and often sent them back after scrawling in the margins *WRONG, WRONG, WRONG* or *SAD, SAD, SAD.*

My brother would have cast his ballot for the current president. Despite my appeals to their Christian sensibilities before the election, I'm pretty sure my brother's wife and children cast their lot on the dark side. *Families!* God help us.

None of us likes to take sides in our family, in our church, or in our nation. I'd rather not. It makes me very uncomfortable. But when sides are drawn, we must choose. And when competing visions and agendas for our nation clash, we must choose.

Before the election I did not declare publicly for any side. Ministers and churches (and tax-exempt publication like this one) are forbidden by law to endorse a party or a candidate during an election. At the National Prayer Breakfast, the president threatened to "destroy" that law. I happen to respect that law and have always honored it.

But now the election is over.

Yes, we must somehow love the president and be kind, but that doesn't mean we condone inflammatory rhetoric, hurtful policies, or attacks on the ideals that make America truly great. Patriots can't remain silent. We stand with the Statue of Liberty. We must not let that torch fall.

The president claims to lead "a historic movement the likes of which the world has never seen." Its marching orders are: *"America First." The rest of the world be damned.*

But no nation is an "island" entirely unto itself. No nation can thrive alone any more than the human species can thrive alone on this planet. To dismiss or discount our interdependency within the web of life or within the family of nations is naive, foolish, and dangerous.

And yet "America First" is now heralded across our land, and patriotism is demanded. But love of country hardly requires a commandment. Patriotism is a natural and honorable affection for one's own country. When patriotism *anywhere* is married to bigotry and belligerence, it is dangerous and abhorrent. It quickly leads to nationalism.

Furthermore, "America First" evokes a dark and shameful era when America refused to join other nations in resisting Hitler and turned away Jewish refugees fleeing the Holocaust. That's taking a side.

I am not on that side.

I am on the side of another historic movement, a movement launched by Jesus in the Sermon on the Mount and shaped by the deep tradition of the Hebrew prophets like Micah. Its marching orders are: *"Love First." May all nations be blessed.*

Taking sides is nothing new. Even Jesus took one side against others. As a first-century Jew under the occupation of the brutal and oppressive Roman Empire, Jesus faced four competing sides, representing four different political postures and strategies.

The Zealots said: We must fight the enemy with fire. Take up weapons and kill the enemy. *No,* said Jesus. *That's not for me. Violence only breeds more violence.*

The Essenes said: We can't win; it's hopeless. So let's run away, hide in the desert, pray and hope for the best. *No,* said Jesus. *I'm not hiding.*

The Sadducees said: We can't beat 'em, so let's join 'em. Let's work in the Green Zone with the Romans. Swallow your dignity and integrity. Be safe. Get rich. *No,* said Jesus. *I will not betray my integrity or my people.*

The Pharisees said: We can't win. Resisting is futile and compromising with infidels is demeaning, so suck it up. Let's live within society but unto ourselves, make our own lives holy and pure and leave the rest to God. *No,* said Jesus. *Holiness, piety, patriotism, and even integrity are not enough.*

Jesus refused to take any of those sides. Those four sides are with us today. They just have different names and slogans.

In the Sermon on the Mount, Jesus proclaimed a new way forward. He launched a revolutionary countermovement against the violent, racist, misogynistic, xenophobic movements that, to his great sorrow, many of his own people embraced.

Jesus said: *Blessed are the merciful. Blessed are the peacemakers. Love your neighbor as yourself, and while you're at it, love your enemy, too. You are the salt of the earth. You are the light of the world. Let your light shine.*

I'm on that side.

And I'm pretty sure many of you are, too, whatever your "faith" may be. It's not about religion. It's about a revolutionary movement of love.

This movement harbors no illusions of easy success. It expects resistance, even fierce persecution and cruel mockery, for the forces of fear, greed, xenophobia, racism, sexism, misogyny, and hate are strong and persistent.

Yes, it's OK to stand up and shout. It's OK to urge the president and other national leaders to respect all peoples and nations and to protest when they don't. It's more than OK. It's necessary. And it's what love requires.

So, please, let your little light shine. Hold it high.

I know, I know. You may feel self-righteous doing so. *But if you wait for moral perfection, you'll never do any good.*

So while holding up your little light, by all means, work on being humble. And while you're working on humility, for heaven's sake, keep standing up. ❧

LET LOVE ARISE

(Dedicated to my mother)

I called through your door,
"The mystics are gathering in the street.
Come out!"

"Leave me alone. I'm sick."

"I don't care if you're dead!
Jesus is here, and he wants to resurrect somebody!"
— RUMI, 13TH-CENTURY PERSIAN SUFI MUSLIM POET

When I was a child, I thought like a child. I thought the resurrection of Jesus proved there was life after death for those who believed in Jesus, and so when I died I would go to heaven and play on streets of gold, because at age 7, I had "accepted Jesus as my personal Lord and Savior." That's how you got in. Or so I was told.

I was a child. I thought like a child, so "heaven and hell" made sense to me. After all, I learned "punishment and reward" from my father's hand, so I figured the "Heavenly Father" operated the same way, with hell as punishment, heaven as reward.

One of my favorite songs back then went like this: *This world is not my home, I'm just a-passin' through; my treasures are laid up somewhere beyond the blue. The angels beckon me from heaven's open door. And I can't feel at home in this world anymore.*

Millions of Christians have sung that ditty, or ones like it, for a hundred years or more. I guess that's why the church of my childhood couldn't care less about making this world more just, peaceable, beautiful, or holy. We were bound for heaven. Earth was a mere launching pad.

When I was a child, I thought like a child. My main worry about heaven was the dress code. From what I could see from pictures in my Sunday school class, the citizens of heaven wore stupid white gowns and played harps all day long for eternity, which sounded like a really long time to be doing something you hated.

I was a child. I thought like a child. I didn't want to wear a white gown or play on a harp. I liked baseball and blue jeans.

So I took my worries to the best authority I knew on that subject: my mother. "I don't want to go to heaven if I can't wear blue jeans and play baseball," I told her.

She assured me that if wearing blue jeans and playing baseball made me happy, there'd be plenty of both in heaven. The jeans would never wear out, and I'd never strike out, she told me. After that, I was all in with heaven.

That may have been the moment I became a progressive theologian. I realized there was more than one way of seeing things, including heaven and the Bible.

I am no longer a child. I see things differently.

I'm not sure about a heaven out there. But I am certain about heaven here on earth. I've experienced it more than once, and I'm guessing you have, too, when everything is just right in your world.

I'm not sure about a heaven up there somewhere. Nor am I sure about a hell beneath us somewhere.

But I am certain about hell on earth. I've experienced that, too, and I'm guessing so have you, when everything feels broken and miserable, as though you've fallen into a cavern of tormenting despair.

Far too many people are living in hell here and now for us to worry about hell somewhere else. When a suicide bomber or the most powerful military force in the world can rain down death and destruction anytime, anywhere, hell is never far away. When the poor, the sick, and the hungry are left to die, hell has arrived.

I now see that heaven and hell are better adjectives than nouns. And I have a different favorite song. It's no longer, "This World Is Not My Home." My favorite song is "Imagine," by John Lennon.

Imagine there's no heaven
It's easy if you try
No hell below us
Above us only sky
Imagine all the people living for today

I once thought that song silly and naive, but I now believe Lennon got it right. We must find a way to live fully in this moment, not for some pie-in-the-sky by and by. We must learn to *be here now*—fully in love with all people, all creatures great and small, and the whole blessed earth.

We must work to make this world whole, beautiful, free, just, peaceable, and good and leave the unknown future in the hands of the One who breathed it all into being. If you've got to worry about things, don't worry about heaven or hell. Worry about social injustice, inequality, poverty, and war here and now.

Imagine no possessions
I wonder if you can
No need for greed or hunger
A brotherhood of man
Imagine all the people sharing all the world.

And in my book, that's where the resurrection of Jesus comes into play. We need that resurrection story—and others—to awaken our imagination.

When I was a child, I thought like a child. Now I see things differently. I imagine a new world.

I'm not so sure the flesh and bones of Jesus skipped out of a tomb on Easter morning. Many people are sure about that; my mother was among them. But, as she taught me, there's more than one way to see things.

Life has evolved on this planet over 4.5 billion years from simple forms into more and more complex forms and into larger and larger communities of interdependency. The wondrous web of life! And evolution ain't done yet! A new creation is on the rise. And as the 14th-century Sufi Muslim poet Hafiz put it: *Nothing evolves us like love.*

The evolution of human consciousness and possibilities can be seen in the life, death, and resurrection of Jesus. That gospel story vindicates not the violent way of empire but the way of Jesus, the way of love. It's an uprising of love in the face of hate. All are welcome. None are turned away.

Let love arise. ❧

JUNE 2019
(2 years after retirement)

THIS LITTLE LIGHT OF MINE

Lately, I've been thinking about writing. About missing it, actually. For 40 years before I retired, I wrote a sermon nearly every week and an essay every three months for the Good News Paper. That's 2,000 sermons and more than 100 essays.

People listened to what I said. People read what I wrote. I heard cheers and boos. I was relevant and didn't even know I was relevant until someone asked me soon after my retirement how it felt to be irrelevant.

I wasn't sure whether that was an insult or a joke. But I took that question into my cave. I sat down, sighed, and unwound. After 40 years of being in the arena, I quickly got used to being in a cave. It was bliss.

And then one day, out of the blue, the devil found me.

You know you used to be somebody. But now you're irrelevant. Looks like you're hiding your light under a bushel, and I like that because when you were letting it shine you gave me fits with your relentless chattering and scribbling about peace, love, and understanding. Stupid people fell for that crap but I wanted to throw up. Such garbage. I hope you rot in this cave and never write a single word again.

The devil left in a huff. But he left a gift.

I started whistling. *This little light of mine I'm gonna let it shine. Hide it under a bushel? No! Never!* I had forgotten how much I loved that song.

Yes, of course, your light may be small—but it's yours. Who knows how or why that light gets in us? It just does. One day, out of the blue, you see something in yourself you'd not seen before.

One day at South High School in Youngstown, Ohio, my 11th grade English teacher, a certain devilish Mr. Ted Moore, said to the class: *Take out a clean sheet of paper and write a 300-word essay entitled "Time." You have 30 minutes.*

Thirty minutes! 1,800 seconds. Half an hour. 1/48th of a day. I was good at math. I wasn't good at creative writing. I could write a book report. I could not make things up out of thin air.

I scrawled "Time" on the top of my paper and stared at it. I slowly underlined the title and added a period after it and then darkened it a little more—a most emphatic period that should have been a most emphatic question mark.

Tick tock tick tock tick tock.

For the first time in my school career that feeling of "I think I'm going to pee my pants any minute now" seized me. I mean, really, who knows what time is? Sure, we know what time it is. But what is time? Who thinks about such things?

Nobody had an inkling what to write. We were 15-year-old kids for cryin' out loud. Any second now we'd all throw up our hands, claim stupidity, and plead for mercy. Of course we would. Any second now.

Tick tock tick tock tick tock.

I looked around at my mates only to see every last one of them leaning over their desks, writing fiercely. *Scratch scratch. Erase erase. Scratch scratch.* What did they know that I didn't?

I looked at the clock. The large hand jerked forward. Time was passing. I could see that. I could feel it. I couldn't stop it.

Tick tock tick tock tick tock.

I stared at my blank paper. I tapped and twirled my pencil. 10 minutes gone. Blank. 15 minutes gone. Blank. 20 minutes gone. Blank. 10 minutes left. I felt time judging my whole reputation as a top-notch student.

Tick tock tick tock tick tock.

I gripped my pencil, licked sweat off my upper lip, gritted my teeth, held my breath, and blindly drove my pencil onto the paper, little knowing that would pretty much be my experience of writing for the next 50 years.

The bell rang. I handed in my paper.

Two days later Mr. Moore returned our essays. He trod up and down the rows slapping down a marked and graded paper on each desk. Everyone got theirs back except me. What?! Had he lost mine?

Mr. Moore returned to his desk. *You all did quite well,* he said. But one essay stood out above the rest. *I'd like to read Randy's.*

I didn't become a writer that day or the next. I brushed it off as sheer luck to have muddled through.

I'm not sure anyone becomes anything in a day or two or even in a year or two. We're always becoming. It takes time for all that's good in us to arise. It takes time. It takes opportunities.

Seeds constantly blow about in the wind. Some fall on hard ground, some among thistles. But now and then one falls on fertile ground, takes root, and blossoms.

So devil beware. I'm stepping out. I'm gripping my pencil. I'm getting back in the arena. I will bring prosperity to West Virginia, democracy back to America, and peace to the world.

But first I need to take a nap. ❧

ABOUT THE AUTHOR

Randall Tremba was born and raised in Youngstown, Ohio. He took a bachelor of arts in philosophy at Wheaton College, Illinois (1969), a master's of divinity at Fuller Theological Seminary, Pasadena, California (1973), and a doctor of ministry at Princeton Seminary (1992). He was installed as minister of the Shepherdstown (WV) Presbyterian Church in July 1976. Forty-one years later he retired. In between he married Paula, became a parent (Jonah, Nathanael, Amanda) and a grandfather, founded the Rumsey Radio Hour (1990), and co-founded the *Shepherdstown Good News Paper* with Ed Zahniser (May 1979). You can follow the author on his blog, thedevilsgift.com.